Competition and Restraint in Cyberspace

The Role of International Norms in Promoting U.S. Cybersecurity

MICHAEL J. MAZARR, BRYAN FREDERICK, EMILY ELLINGER, BENJAMIN BOUDREAUX

Prepared for the Office of the Secretary of Defense
Approved for public release; distribution unlimited

RAND NATIONAL DEFENSE RESEARCH INSTITUTE

For more information on this publication, visit **www.rand.org/t/RRA1180-1**.

About RAND

The RAND Corporation is a research organization that develops solutions to public policy challenges to help make communities throughout the world safer and more secure, healthier and more prosperous. RAND is nonprofit, nonpartisan, and committed to the public interest. To learn more about RAND, visit www.rand.org.

Research Integrity

Our mission to help improve policy and decisionmaking through research and analysis is enabled through our core values of quality and objectivity and our unwavering commitment to the highest level of integrity and ethical behavior. To help ensure our research and analysis are rigorous, objective, and nonpartisan, we subject our research publications to a robust and exacting quality-assurance process; avoid both the appearance and reality of financial and other conflicts of interest through staff training, project screening, and a policy of mandatory disclosure; and pursue transparency in our research engagements through our commitment to the open publication of our research findings and recommendations, disclosure of the source of funding of published research, and policies to ensure intellectual independence. For more information, visit www.rand.org/about/principles.

RAND's publications do not necessarily reflect the opinions of its research clients and sponsors.

Published by the RAND Corporation, Santa Monica, Calif.

Library of Congress Cataloging-in-Publication Data is available for this publication.
ISBN: 978-1-9774-0731-3

Cover image: Pavel/Getty Images.

About This Report

In this report, the authors examine the recent history of and future potential for normative constraints on aggressive and disruptive cyber activity. Recent years have seen a mounting concern in the United States over foreign efforts to harm election security or legitimacy through cyber means, an increase in cyber espionage, and attacks of growing sophistication. The United States has been engaged for almost a decade in international negotiations over agreed normative constraints on such activities.

The research for the report was performed, and is limited to facts and data available, from late 2019 through the end of 2020.

The research reported here was completed in April 2021 and underwent security review with the sponsor and the Defense Office of Prepublication and Security Review before public release.

RAND Corporation National Security Research Division

This research was sponsored by the Office of the Secretary of Defense and conducted within the Cyber and Intelligence Policy Center of the RAND Corporation National Security Research Division (NSRD), which operates the National Defense Research Institute (NDRI), a federally funded research and development center sponsored by the Office of the Secretary of Defense, the Joint Staff, the Unified Combatant Commands, the Navy, the Marine Corps, the defense agencies, and the defense intelligence enterprise. For more information on the Cyber and

Intelligence Policy Center, see www.rand.org/nsrd/intel.html or contact the director (contact information is provided on the webpage).

Acknowledgments

We extend our grateful thanks to Rich Girven, director of the Cyber and Intelligence Policy Center, for his support of the research. In addition to the named coauthors, we thank our former RAND colleague Jared Ellinger as well as Alexander Klimburg and Tim Sweijs for very useful conversations on these issues, though they are not responsible for any of the conclusions or recommendations in this report. We have benefited from participation in parallel studies on cyber stability and norm development directed by our RAND colleague Samuel Charap and by Tim Sweijs.

Contents

Table

Summary

Issue

Recent years have seen a growing concern in the United States of foreign efforts to harm election security or legitimacy through cyber means, as well as cyber espionage and attacks of growing sophistication. The United States has been engaged for almost a decade in international negotiations over agreed normative constraints on such activities. This research, the product of internally funded RAND Corporation research support, examined the history of and prospects for such constraints.

Approach

First, surveying the literature on norms and norm emergence, the report describes the process by which norms tend to arise. It then reviews the history of intergovernmental and private-sector initiatives on cyber norms, outlines the principles governing U.S. government policy on the issue since 2007, and surveys current proposals for cyber norms. Based on this analysis, the authors propose a renewed agenda for the United States that bypasses current international disagreements to encourage the development of norms to constrain the most destructive and escalatory forms of cyber aggression.

Primary Findings

Our research produced several primary findings on the character of and prospects for cyber norms. First, there is no clear, emerging consensus on the precise shape of required norms. While some principles are common to several global aspirational statements, none has achieved formal recognition and promised enforcement by all the major cyber powers, all of whom continue to act with a significant degree of cyber impunity.

Second, the gap on these issues between the United States and both China and Russia remains very wide, and there is limited room for mutually agreed restraints on behavior. It is not clear whether any of these powers are willing to agree to enough mutual, voluntary restrictions on their freedom of action in cyberspace to make a broader regime of cyber norms possible.

Third, cyberspace also has specific characteristics that may impede the development of norms to restrict state behavior. The nature and complexity of cyberspace, for example, makes attribution of actions much more difficult than in other domains, and attribution is a key requirement for imposing costs for any violations of potential cyber norms.

Fourth, however, it is important to neither exaggerate the degree of destabilizing cyber behavior nor underestimate the fact that some implicit norms may—gradually—be emerging even as major cyber espionage and intrusion events continue. No major cyber power has launched widespread destructive hacks on another. The United States, Russia, and China each have legitimate reasons to support some constraints on cyber aggression. The best example of this emerging progress is a consistent emphasis in recent intergovernmental cyber norm statements, endorsed by all major cyber powers, on mutual nonaggression against critical national infrastructure.

Fifth, our review of the character of international norms in other fields offers several lessons for building norms in cyberspace:

- Norms can affect state behavior even where national leaders openly disagree with the content of those norms. Norms derive their ability to shape state behavior primarily from how they affect the expectations and behavior of the broader international or domestic societies in which states operate. Individual leader belief in the rightness of a given norm can of course be helpful in promoting or strengthening a norm, but it is not required.

- Norms can become established through "bottom-up" efforts, through the work of experts, nongovernmental organizations (NGOs), and civil society more broadly, rather than being negotiated or imposed by governments. In areas where governmental consensus may be elusive, this history highlights potential alternative pathways for norms to become established.
- Effective norms tend to be simple rather than complex, emotive rather than dry, and framed around avoiding risk to innocent life rather than more abstract considerations. All of these characteristics, however, pose challenges to developing norms to govern behavior in cyberspace. Many types of cyber behavior that policymakers may wish to prohibit or restrain can be highly technical in nature and may be difficult to observe.

Sixth and finally, the current status of international discussions does not provide the basis for believing that any large-scale agreements on cyber norms are feasible in the near term. Despite some progress, including the most recent report of the UN Group of Governmental Experts (GGE) in May 2021, the most fundamental issue under dispute—the claim of autocratic regimes like China and Russia of a right to control their "information borders" in a form of cyber sovereignty—does not seem able to be resolved through negotiation. One implication is that the recurrent Russian proposal to reach a general treaty constraining such activities, perhaps grounded in international law, is likely not in the cards. The perspectives of major powers are simply not well enough aligned to support such a treaty, and the negotiations over one are likely to bog down into debates that return to fundamental differences in perspective.

This analysis suggests that rather than a "top-down," "inside-out" option built around a formalized agreement among the major cyber powers, the United States may have greater success with a more bottom-up, "outside-in" strategy of building gradual momentum for norms that it perceives to be most essential. Such an approach would begin with an effort to establish a set of clear principles that the United

States believes should be "beyond the pale" in cyberspace; and then use diplomacy, support for nongovernmental processes, and collaboration with NGOs, private companies, and like-minded states to gain widespread international and public support for those norms. The May 2021 GGE report and related intergovernmental statements, as well as public signaling during the June 2021 U.S.-Russia summit, represent the sort of steps that such a gradual, emergent approach to norm building can build on.

An Agenda for Renewed Progress

This report then outlines a possible agenda to pursue such a bottom-up, outside-in strategy, while still deepening ongoing dialogues with Russia and China and laying the groundwork for possible future cyber norms among those major cyber actors. The agenda has three stages.

Stage 1: Clearing the Way for Progress

A first step is to bring U.S. policy into line with a regime of growing constraints on cyber attacks. This can include a recognition that while the U.S. position is that international law applies in cyberspace, it recognizes that not all states agree with that interpretation, and this dispute should not obstruct other progress. More important, this stage would also involve constraints on certain U.S. offensive cyber activities. The United States could announce an initial set of standards of conduct for state behavior in the cyber realm that the United States will seek to establish and by which it intends to abide. By offering to "go first" in specifying and abiding by the restrictions on illegitimate behavior in the cyber realm that it proposes, the United States would have the opportunity first to define these restrictions in a manner likely to anchor future discussion and development of them, as well as to build diplomatic and political support for the restrictions through its own example.

Such openness to constraints on U.S. behavior is a critical component of any effort to rein in the employment of cyber tools. If the United States (or U.S. allies and partners) employs offensive cyber means more widely, it risks creating a pattern of state behavior suggesting that any norms in this area will not be reliably observed. An important step for this effort to build trust, credibility, and leadership should involve a senior-level speech that clearly lays out the criteria that govern U.S. cyber operations.

Stage 2: Continuing Initiatives

The new administration could also continue with and enhance various initiatives already underway in the cyber norms area. These steps could include the following:

- Publicly reemphasize the importance of emerging norms in this area.
- Feature cyber norms in discussions with democratic allies and partners on a reinvigorated U.S. multilateralism.
- Beyond state practice, support intergovernmental, public-private, and nongovernmental organizations and processes designed to ratify the commitment of various coalitions of stakeholders to emergent cyber norms and expand their public profile and attention.
- Act to impose costs on states that violate emerging cyber norms.
- Reaffirm and expand confidence-building mechanisms with Russia and China.

Stage 3: New Initiatives

Finally, the new administration can develop an agenda of actions designed to make tangible progress within its first two years. These actions could include the following:

- Organize for cyber norm promotion: Gain congressional approval of an institutional home within the U.S. government for the process of cyber norm development.
- Enunciate bilateral, informal commitments with other powers to refrain from certain categories of cyber aggression in ways that help reinforce emergent norms.
- Propose a standing working group with either Russia or China (or both) to allow experts and government officials to build on the recent intergovernmental statements, discuss issues, and slowly build toward limited areas of consensus, and to develop rules of engagement and communication mechanisms to handle cyber disputes.
- Convene new multilateral intergovernmental, and multistakeholder, processes to gather a critical mass of partners in the effort.

Identifying Specific Normative Constraints for General Agreement

As the final component of its new initiatives, the new administration should make a powerful public commitment to the foundational norms at the core of its early effort, while making clear that they are simply initial priorities and do not exhaust the scope of normative constraint that can emerge in this domain. Based on considerations of urgency, and also drawing on lessons from our review of the development of other norms (which indicated that simpler, more absolute norms—as well as those with relatively clear linkages to human welfare—are more likely to spread and become established), our analysis suggests the following three major normative initiatives as promising early focus for U.S. attention:

- Complete prohibitions on any cyber attacks on critical infrastructure, either essential or significant
- Prohibitions on direct interference in or manipulation of election and political processes
- Prohibitions on activity designed to intentionally and substantially damage the availability or integrity of the public core of the internet, including the basic domain-name system as well as central server locations and primary avenues of data transmission.

These areas of focus represent what we assess to be the most promising and urgent places to begin in efforts to promote cyber norms. Should these initial efforts gain traction, the United States could also expand its efforts on a wider front to establish a more comprehensive set of cyber norms, first among democracies and then more broadly. Combined with the investment in catalytic, multistakeholder efforts toward cyber norm emergence described above, they would constitute an agenda designed to make as much progress as possible toward greater cyber stability in an admittedly constraining international context.

Abbreviations

CBM	confidence-building measure
CSIRT	computer security incident response team
DPRK	Democratic People's Republic of Korea
G20	Group of 20
GGE	group of governmental experts
ICT	information and communication technology
NGO	nongovernmental organization
OEWG	open-ended working group
U.N.	United Nations

CHAPTER ONE

The Challenge of Norms in Cyberspace

Great powers compete with one another across multiple domains to secure their interests and promote their security. In recent years, perhaps the most dramatic area of rising competition has been in cyberspace, where these states have pursued widely divergent strategies of competition, including some that appear to be highly risky or destabilizing for international security. The scope and variety of cyber-enabled means of competition has been expanding to include such activities as meddling in democratic processes and the theft of industrial secrets at an increasing scale and level of sophistication. Major powers are also seeking ways to wage large-scale, destructive forms of conflict through virtual means.[1] More than almost any other area of competition, such tools have the potential to threaten the stability of major power relations by creating direct threats to political and economic security in national homelands.[2]

---

[1] Joseph S. Nye, "Normative Restraints on Cyber Conflict," Harvard University Belfer Center, August 2018; and Michael J. Mazarr, Ryan Michael Bauer, Abigail Casey, Sarah Heintz, and Luke J. Matthews, *The Emerging Risk of Virtual Societal Warfare: Social Manipulation in a Changing Information Environment*, Santa Monica, Calif.: RAND Corporation, RR-2714-OSD, 2019.

[2] It is worth noting that there is an academic debate regarding the risks of cyber conflict itself to escalate beyond the cyber realm into kinetic warfare. Valeriano, Jensen, and Maness, for example, argue that the risks of escalation from the cyber domain to conventional war or conflict are quite limited, treating cyber attacks as essentially the new form of traditional espionage. By contrast, Schneider and others argue that the potential escalation risks are much more substantial. While this report is not intended to be a review of this debate, we do argue, below, that cyber attacks can have broader effects on the political or economic fortunes of states, and particularly in this way they run the risk of escalating conflicts. See Brandon Valeriano, Benjamin Jensen, and Ryan C. Maness, *Cyber Strategy: The Evolving Character of Power and Coercion*, New York, Oxford University Press, 2018, p. 204; Jacquelyn Schneider, "A Strategic Cyber No-First-Use Policy? Addressing the US Cyber Strategy Problem," *Washington Quarterly* Vol. 43, No. 2, 2020, pp. 160–164.

Already widely accepted as fact, the growing risk posed by cyber threats to national security was powerfully reinforced in the December 2020 revelations about the alleged Russian SolarWinds cyber espionage campaign, in which access to a third-party vendor's software was used to gain access to dozens of government and private-sector information systems.[3] Although this was a case of cyber espionage, at least so far, and not a direct attack using cyber means, it nonetheless generated multiple calls in the United States to retaliate in some way. The event demonstrated once again the general risk, as well as escalatory potential, of cyber aggression.

Investments in cyber resilience and threats of punishment will be part of the U.S. response to such dangers. Indeed, they are likely to become, and remain, the primary tools of statecraft for promoting cybersecurity. In other domains of competition, however, the United States has frequently used formally or informally agreed rules of the road and multilateral norms to help constrain the destabilizing aspects of competition and create a context in which policies of deterrence and defense would be more effective. Such rules and norms have ranged from elaborate arms control treaties to rules of engagement in the air and on the high seas to unwritten rules that nonetheless restrict state behavior, such as the norm against the use of nuclear weapons.

The recent U.S. Cyberspace Solarium Commission—a bipartisan commission established by Congress to develop a consensus strategic approach to cyberspace—emphasized the potential utility of norms as part of a broader "layered deterrence" approach to cyber threats. "While unilateral activity can provide the greatest short-term flexibility," the commission concluded, "norms-based multilateral engagement provides a more effective means to reduce the likelihood and effectiveness of cyberattacks." The commission contended that this was true for at least three reasons: "Norms can change an adversary's decision calculus"; a multilateral system of norms "reduces the burden on any one nation to enforce the system of norms"; and "frameworks

---

[3] David E. Sanger, Nicole Perlroth, and Julian E. Barnes, "Billions Spent on U.S. Defenses Failed to Detect Giant Russian Hack," *New York Times*, December 16, 2020; and Alex Ward, "How the U.S. Government Attack Happened, and What It Means," *Vox*, December 18, 2020.

of norms are sticky—once a pattern of behavior is set, it becomes difficult to dislodge."[4]

The issue became even more timely in May and June 2021, with the release of the latest United Nations Group of Governmental Experts (GGE) report on cyber norms and the proposals for norms raised in the June summit between Presidents Joe Biden and Vladimir Putin. Those processes and statements touch on some of the recommendations we make in this report. Mainly, however, they set the stage for a new chapter of U.S. efforts to promote such norms.

A crucial question is whether such rules and norms can help moderate the cyber competition in ways that meaningfully protect U.S. interests. Governments, scholars, nongovernmental organizations (NGOs), and private-sector companies have made dozens of proposals for rules and norms to govern cyber activities, including some grounded in international law. The U.S. government has for several years been engaged in multiple international forums to advance the goal of building cyber norms.[5] It is not obvious how or why additional efforts by the new Biden administration would have more significant results.

While some principles are common to several global aspirational statements, none has achieved formal recognition and promised enforcement by all the major cyber powers, all of which continue to act with a significant degree of cyber impunity. It is not clear whether any of these powers are willing to agree to *enough* mutual, voluntary restrictions on their freedom of action in cyberspace to make a broader cyber norms regime possible. The gap on these issues between the United States and both China and Russia remains very wide, and there is limited room for mutually agreed restraints on behavior.

Cyberspace also has specific characteristics that may impede the development of norms to restrict state behavior. The requirements of information security, and therefore state cyber capabilities and vulnerabilities, are constantly changing, complicating the task of identify-

---

4 U.S. Cyberspace Solarium Commission, *Final Report*, March 2020, p. 46.

5 Joseph Marks, "U.S. Makes New Push for Global Rules in Cyberspace," *Politico*, May 5, 2015.

ing durable norms.[6] If too detailed or technical in nature, norms in cyberspace could achieve widespread consensus only to become obsolete or superseded by new technologies or approaches. The nature and complexity of cyberspace also makes attribution of actions much more difficult than in other domains, and attribution is a key requirement for imposing costs for any violations of potential cyber norms. Absent clear, publicly releasable, and understandable evidence to support attribution, other states and actors might be hesitant to impose costs on violators solely based on the analysis or assessment of the victim.[7]

At the same time, it is important not to exaggerate the degree of destabilizing cyber behavior or to underestimate the fact that some implicit norms may—gradually—be emerging even as major cyber espionage and intrusion events continue. No major cyber power has launched widespread destructive hacks on another. While states probe and gather information on each other's governmental, political, and other critical infrastructure, a significant degree of escalation restraint appears to be holding for the time being in the cyber realm. These are reflected, at least in the U.S. case, by a set of commitments that have become known as the "peacetime norms" on cyber issues, which are embedded in multiple international documents.[8] A form of deterrence may be coalescing in this domain, empowered by the simple fact that if cyber aggression becomes destructive enough, the victims reserve the right to answer it with kinetic strikes. Despite almost daily news of new cyber thefts and intrusions, and very high-profile hacks like the SolarWinds event, it may well be that a modest set of norms governing restraint in cyberspace is indeed taking root.

This report assesses the potential for and feasibility of expanded and accelerated rule and norm building in the cyber realm. To set the

---

[6] Global Commission on the Stability of Cyberspace, *Advancing Cyberstability*, Final Report, Hague Center for Strategic Studies and EastWest Institute, November 2019, p. 23.

[7] Of course, noting that these factors may make norms more difficult to establish in cyberspace should not be understood to imply that other factors, such as political or strategic concerns that affect state calculations, may not play an even larger role in the success or failure of cyber norms. This issue is discussed in detail in Chapter Three.

[8] See, for example, U.S. Department of State, "Joint Statement on Advancing Responsible State Behavior in Cyberspace," September 23, 2019.

context, it assesses how the cyber strategies pursued by the United States, Russia, and China fit with their strategies of competition with one another more broadly. It briefly reviews available evidence about why these states have chosen the cyber strategies they have.

The report evaluates the potential of specific rules and norms that moderate the cyber competition in several ways. In this report, we

- explore the costs and benefits that have accrued to the major cyber powers from the choices they have made in order to gain a sense of their interests and possible motives for restraint
- discuss the general challenge of rule and norm building in the cyber arena, particularly the problems of attribution, verification, and enforcement
- review and evaluate existing proposals for rules and norms, judging them against the apparent objectives and interests of the major cyber powers
- determine whether any discrete package of rules and norms seems most feasible as an initial goal for U.S. policymakers to pursue; and evaluate the detailed interests, policies, and statements of the major powers against these options. We further assess whether linkage between compliance with cyber rules or norms and leverage or concessions in other domains might be a plausible means of reaching agreement.

Subsequent chapters discuss each of these themes. Chapter Two explores how international norms operate and come to be formed and explores possible historical examples of other international norms that could illustrate ways in which cyber norms could develop. Chapter Three situates cyber norm issues within the broader strategic calculations of three key states—the United States, Russia, and China—and reviews the extensive efforts made to date by states, international organizations, and other actors, including international legal experts and the private sector, to propose or develop cyber norms. Chapter Four analyzes the present state of the development of cyber norms and provides our assessment of the most promising ways forward.

CHAPTER TWO

Understanding Norms

International norms may appear to be a challenging means by which to restrain the behavior of China and Russia and promote stability in cyberspace. These states, after all, have routinely violated international standards on issues such as human rights, arms control, and international aggression.[1] Norms, particularly in an area such as cyber, where state behavior that might violate such norms is difficult to verify, would seem to be a problematic tool to use to modify Russian and Chinese behavior.

This chapter lays out the theoretical case for why and how norms may be a useful means of restraining competition in cyberspace and promoting stability. It defines norms in general terms, explains how they tend to become established, and describes the means by which they can be used to modify the behavior of states, even those states that may disagree with their prescriptions. It then provides examples of other norms that have led to changes in state behavior and highlights the conditions on which their apparent success seems to have depended. Following a review of major cyber power positions and current negotiation efforts in Chapter Three, in Chapter Four we discuss in detail how cyber norms in the present context might be developed and assess their prospects for effectiveness.

---

[1] Lindsay Maizland, "China's Repression of Uighurs in Xinjiang," Council on Foreign Relations, June 30, 2020; North Atlantic Council, "Statement on Russia's Failure to Comply with the Intermediate-Range Nuclear Forces (INF) Treaty," February 1, 2019; and Thomas Grant, "Russia's Invasion of Ukraine: What Does International Law Have to Say?" Lawfare Blog, August 25, 2015.

How Do International Norms Work?

International norms identify behavior that is appropriate for states.[2] This appropriateness is determined socially, both internationally (by the views of other states) and domestically (by the views of domestic publics). By shifting public and international expectations about appropriate behavior for states, international norms can shift state leader calculations regarding the actions they should take.

Well-established norms can alter the perceptions of state leaders regarding the costs they may face if they undertake behaviors that these norms hold to be inappropriate through both international and domestic mechanisms. Internationally, the costs of violating norms may come through diplomatic isolation, reticence to partner with violating states, or other forms of international sanction as other states express their dissatisfaction with the violating state's behavior.[3] Domestically, state leaders that violate norms the public considers to be established may become unpopular, or their governance viewed as illegitimate.[4] Crucially, these costs for state leaders that violate established norms can accrue regardless of whether the leaders themselves agree with the content of these norms. They need only be attuned to

---

[2] Mary Fainsod Katzenstein, *The Culture of National Security: Norms and Identity in World Politics*, New York: Columbia University Press, 1996, p. 5. Some literature on norms distinguishes the notions of appropriateness and behavior; in this analysis, we employ norm conceptions that effectively join the two and speak to the emergence of standards for what is commonly viewed as appropriate or acceptable state behavior. See, for example, Ann Florini, "The Evolution of International Norms," *International Studies Quarterly*, Vol. 40, No. 3, 1996, pp. 364–365; and Annika Björkdahl, "Norms in International Relations: Some Conceptual and Methodological Reflections," *Cambridge Review of International Affairs*, Vol. 15, No. 1, 2002, 13, who concludes that "norms are general prescriptions of behavior which regulate intentions and effects." Stephen Krasner refers to norms as "standards of behavior"; Stephen D. Krasner, "Structural Causes and Regime Consequences: Regimes as Intervening Variables," *International Organization*, Vol. 36, No. 2, 1982, p. 186.

[3] James H. Lebovic and Erik Voeten, "The Cost of Shame: International Organizations and Foreign Aid in the Punishing of Human Rights Violators," *Journal of Peace Research*, Vol. 46, No. 1, 2009, p. 79; Steven Levitsky, and Lucan Way, "International Linkage and Democratization," *Journal of Democracy*, Vol. 16, No. 3, 2005, p. 21.

[4] Sonia Cardenas, "Norm Collision: Explaining the Effects of International Human Rights Pressure on State Behavior," *International Studies Review*, Vol. 6, No. 2, 2004, pp. 215–216.

the costs that violations of the norms would impose in order to have an incentive to follow them.[5]

Most international norms are generally conceived of in a negative sense; they prohibit certain behaviors. But norms can also be thought of in a positive sense; they encourage the adoption of certain behaviors or policies in order for states to be considered responsible actors.[6] While the discussion in this chapter primarily focuses on a negative framing of norms, it is worth noting that both have clear applicability to the cyber realm. Negative norms, for example, might be essential for prohibiting attacks on critical infrastructure that could be highly destabilizing. But positive norms, such as the importance of maintaining transparency and good "cyber hygiene," may also enhance stability. These issues are discussed in greater detail in Chapter Four.

How Do International Norms Become Established?

International norms are generally thought to go through three stages in order to become firmly established. In the first stage of "norm emergence," norms are typically first promoted by "norm entrepreneurs," often individuals or NGOs that identify a state behavior as wrong or inappropriate and promote an alternative rule for behavior that restricts this practice. Their appeals for change are often emotive, focused on the negative consequences of transgressive behavior, and seek to draw attention to those consequences. Norms are more likely to be successful in this stage when they are "clear and specific, rather than ambiguous or complex."[7] Further, successful norms are

---

[5] Of course, if state leaders do share the consensus view embodied in such norms, then the effectiveness of the norms in regulating state behavior becomes further enhanced. In their strongest form, violations of such norms may become almost literally unthinkable, in that state leaders will no longer seriously consider policies that would do so.

[6] Jeffrey T. Checkel, "The Constructivist Turn in International Relations Theory," *World Politics*, Vol. 50, No. 2, 1998, pp. 336–337.

[7] Martha Finnemore and Kathryn Sikkink, "International Norm Dynamics and Political Change," *International Organization*, Vol. 52, No. 4, 1998, p. 907.

often framed in a manner that suggests they aim at the "prevention of bodily harm for vulnerable or 'innocent' groups."[8] Entrepreneurs are also more likely to be successful in convincing key states to support norms when they develop organizations or platforms to support or amplify their messages.[9] States that decide to follow emerging norms may also need to "go first," adopting the restrictions of a norm before their competitors or adversaries do.[10]

States that adopted the norm initially work to encourage the adoption of the norm by other states. These efforts are likely to be effective first in relatively friendly or like-minded states, and to be supported by networks of individuals or NGOs that are also invested in promoting the norm. States may be persuaded to adopt these emerging norms either because of the perceived rightness of the norm, because of the domestic political consequences of either adopting or refusing to adopt the norm, or because of the material logic of doing so.[11] Even in this early stage, norms can begin to affect the behavior of states, and in particular those states relatively similar to the initial norm entrepreneurs or promoters, though they may have less initial effect on the behavior of states that oppose their development.

In the second stage, after a certain number of states, and a certain number of influential or important states, adopt the norm, it can then reach a tipping point after which international pressure grows for other states that have thus far resisted the norm to nonetheless adopt

---

[8] Finnemore and Sikkink, 1998, p. 907.

[9] For example, the efforts of NGOs were instrumental in promoting norms against the use of both landmines and cluster munitions. See Kenneth R. Rutherford, "The Evolving Arms Control Agenda: Implications of the Role of NGOs in Banning Antipersonnel Landmines," *World Politics*, Vol. 53, No. 1, 2000; and Elvira Rosert, "Norm Emergence as Agenda Diffusion: Failure and Success in the Regulation of Cluster Munitions," *European Journal of International Relations*, Vol. 25, No. 4, 2019.

[10] Notably, this logic differs from, for example, Cold War–era nuclear arms control agreements, where a state agrees to restrict its capabilities only *if* the other party to the agreement does so as well.

[11] For example, a state might decide to adopt and promote a norm that would treat a particular military capability that it lacks—but that an adversary has—as illegitimate.

it, resulting in what is often called a "norm cascade."[12] This pressure can be both international, in terms of diplomatic, reputational, or even material (sanctions) costs imposed by some states on others; or it may be domestic, as most publics prefer that their governments are viewed as legitimate and responsible internationally.[13]

In the third and final stage, norms that are successful in achieving widespread adoption can then go through "internalization," wherein they are widely codified into both international agreements and domestic laws.[14] Once internalized in this manner, norms come to be viewed as more or less unquestioned standards of behavior, such that violating them is no longer seriously considered as a policy option by most state leaders, and violations may in any event become increasingly costly or difficult in legal or diplomatic terms.

The first of these three stages, norm emergence, is of greatest interest for this report. There have to date been very few if any norms governing cyber behavior that have emerged from this first stage with the potential to go through the final two stages.[15] While norms in this first stage can have some limited restraining effect on the behavior of states, more firmly established norms are likely to have stronger effects. Our analysis therefore focuses on how norms in cyberspace might be promoted into these latter stages.

---

12 Cass R. Sunstein, "Social Norms and Social Roles," *Columbia Law Review*, Vol. 96, No. 4, 1996, p. 909.

13 Finnemore and Sikkink, 1998, pp. 902–904.

14 Finnemore and Sikkink, 1998, p. 905.

15 For example, while there does appear to be general international agreement regarding the need to prosecute cyber crime, defining the standards and mechanisms by which to do so remains more fragmented, and there seems to be little international pressure to converge toward a single standard. The 2001 Budapest Convention on Cybercrime has been ratified by 65 countries, mostly in Europe, but has seen more limited adoption elsewhere. Most states, including China, Russia, India, Brazil, South Korea, and Mexico, remain outside the treaty. See Council of Europe, "Chart of Signatures and Ratifications of Treaty 185, Convention on Cybercrime," undated; and Louk Faesen, Tim Sweijs, Alexander Klimburg, Conor MacNamara, and Michael Mazarr, *From Blurred Lines to Red Lines: How Countermeasures and Norms Shape Hybrid Conflict*, Hague Centre for Strategic Studies, October 2020, pp. 34–35.

Do Existing International Norms Provide Potential Models for Restraining Cyber Competition?

Several existing international norms that restrict the use of state capabilities provide examples that may have relevance for our consideration of how to establish potential norms to restrict the use of cyber capabilities. In this section, we highlight two: the development of a norm against the use of nuclear weapons (despite widespread continued possession of such weapons among major powers), and the more recent development of a norm against the use of antipersonnel landmines that has resulted in widespread, though not universal, restrictions. These cases, of course, substantially differ in numerous ways from efforts to establish cyber norms, including in the greater physical destructiveness of the capabilities restricted, and in their focus on more categorical restrictions against the use of the weapons involved, rather than proposed restrictions on cyber attacks primarily against certain targets, as discussed in Chapter Four. However, both cases do illustrate important aspects of how different international norms can become established, and in doing so they help illuminate a potential path forward for cyber norms, as discussed below.

The Nuclear "Taboo"

The consistent nonuse of nuclear weapons since 1945 has been a central feature of the modern strategic environment. While states, including most notably the United States, the Soviet Union, and Russia, have amassed tremendous stockpiles of nuclear weapons and these weapons have played a central role in affecting the decisionmaking of key states throughout the past 75 years, they have not been used in any of the myriad conflicts since 1945 in which nuclear states have become embroiled. This nonuse has been supported by a number of factors, including strategic calculations regarding likely adversary reactions to nuclear use, but international norms also appear to have played a key role.

Since the early days of the Cold War, nuclear weapons have been categorized as different in nature from conventional weapons, lumped together with biological and chemical weapons as "weapons of mass destruction" whose use carries moral sanction.[16] Widespread public and elite concern throughout Western democracies, including the United States, after 1945 led to the early stigmatization of the use of nuclear weapons, and to the perception among policymakers that any military benefits from nuclear use would be outweighed by the political and diplomatic costs of doing so.[17] These concerns were amplified by Soviet political and information efforts, as Moscow sought to make unusable this key advantage the United States had over it in the early Cold War period.[18]

While moral concerns regarding the (further) use of nuclear weapons were shared by senior members of the Truman administration during the Korean War, this was not the case for the Eisenhower administration. Both Eisenhower and Secretary of State Dulles viewed nuclear weapons as appropriate warfighting weapons, but they were acutely aware that key allies and the general public did not share this view, and they therefore considered options to fight against this emerging nuclear "taboo" in order to retain U.S. freedom of action.[19] Despite considering potential nuclear use to help end the Korean War and in other Cold War crises throughout the 1950s, they ultimately could not identify any opportunities to do so that would merit the likely costs. By the next major U.S. conflict of the Cold War, Vietnam, nuclear weapons were no longer considered to be a serious warfighting option, despite substantial U.S. losses and, ultimately, defeat.[20] This

---

[16] Chemical weapons, after frequent use in the First World War, were nonetheless avoided by all sides during the Second World War, despite the tremendous stakes involved and the clear willingness to inflict substantial civilian and military casualties. Nina Tannenwald, "Stigmatizing the Bomb: Origins of the Nuclear Taboo," *International Security*, Vol. 29, No. 4, 2005, pp. 18–20.

[17] Lawrence S. Wittner, *The Struggle Against the Bomb: Volume One, One World or None: A History of the World Nuclear Disarmament Movement Through 1953*, Stanford, Calif., Stanford University Press, 1993.

[18] Peter Gizewski, "From Winning Weapon to Destroyer of Worlds: The Nuclear Taboo in International Politics," *International Journal*, Vol. 51, No. 3, 1996, p. 403.

[19] Nina Tannenwald, "The Nuclear Taboo: The United States and the Normative Basis of Nuclear Non-Use," *International Organization*, Vol. 53, No. 3, 1999, pp. 448–450.

[20] Nina Tannenwald, "Nuclear Weapons and the Vietnam War," *Journal of Strategic Studies*, Vol. 29, No. 4, 2006, p. 675.

norm against nuclear use has persisted through later conflicts in which their use could have brought military benefits, such as the 1991 Persian Gulf War.[21]

The norm restricting the use of nuclear weapons—the most destructive weapons ever invented—appears at first glance to have few parallels with contemporary concerns about cyber capabilities, which while they have the potential to lead to loss of life likely have notably lower risks of mass casualties than nuclear weapons. However, the nuclear weapons taboo is a useful example of a norm that emerged to restrict a military capability over the objections of at least one of the key states that possessed that capability. During the Eisenhower administration, senior decisionmakers, including the president, had no wish to be bound by the emerging nuclear taboo, but they found that they were nonetheless subject to political and diplomatic constraints imposed by the norm. This provides a dramatic illustration of the fact that norms have the capability to shape and regulate state behavior whether or not the leaders of those states agree with them. While the United States has maintained a stated commitment to the flexible use of nuclear weapons, and has continuously possessed, maintained, and developed these weapons for decades, it has not used them, despite militarily advantageous opportunities to do so. If advocates of the regulation of cyber capabilities are unsuccessful in persuading the major cyber powers to agree to "disarmament" of potentially destabilizing cyber capabilities, then the nuclear taboo provides an example of how—given sufficient political and diplomatic consensus—incentives to avoid the use of certain cyber capabilities could potentially still be imposed over the objections of some key states.

The International Campaign to Ban Landmines

The second example of the use of a norm to restrict state capabilities offers a more complex picture, and a different set of lessons. The 1990s saw the development and widespread adoption of an international norm to ban the use of antipersonnel landmines. Such landmines had been widely deployed in numerous Cold War–era conflicts, and their presence even after the end of such conflicts led to continuing, wide-

[21] Tannenwald, 1999, pp. 458–462.

spread civilian casualties, including some 15,000–20,000 in 2002.[22] Only 15 percent of casualties from landmines were estimated to involve military personnel.[23]

A potential ban on antipersonnel landmines was originally attempted through international negotiations surrounding the Additional Protocols to the Geneva Conventions in 1977, and their use explicitly against civilians was banned by the 1980 Convention on Certain Conventional Weapons.[24] However, these documents had little effect on the use of antipersonnel mines in practice. By the early 1990s, a collection of influential NGOs, including most notably Human Rights Watch and the International Committee of the Red Cross, created an umbrella organization called the International Campaign to Ban Landmines (ICBL) to advocate for a complete, global ban on the use of the weapons.[25]

The ICBL pursued a strategy of public and elite engagement to lobby for states to stop using the weapons and to produce a new international agreement codifying a ban. The campaign was eventually joined by more than 1,000 NGOs, ranging from large, international organizations to localized, grassroots organizations across the world; collectively, their involvement greatly expanded the reach and influence of the campaign.[26] This resulted by 1997 in the Ottawa Convention (or the "Convention on the Prohibition of the Use, Stockpiling, Production and Transfer of Anti-Personnel Mines and on Their Destruction"), in which roughly 80 percent of the states in the world

---

[22] Toran Hansen, "The Campaign to Ban Landmines," *Peace Review*, Vol. 16, No. 3, 2004, p. 365.

[23] Hansen, 2004, p. 365.

[24] Charli R. Carpenter, "Vetting the Advocacy Agenda: Network Centrality and the Paradox of Weapons Norms," *International Organization*, Vol. 65, No. 1, January 2011, p. 85; and United Nations, *Convention on Prohibitions or Restrictions on the Use of Certain Conventional Weapons Which May Be Deemed to Be Excessively Injurious or to Have Indiscriminate Effects: Protocol on Prohibitions or Restrictions on the Use of Mines, Booby-Traps and Other Devices: Protocol II*, October 10, 1980.

[25] Carpenter, 2011, pp. 85–86.

[26] Lesley Wexler, "The International Deployment of Shame, Second-Best Responses, and Norm Entrepreneurship: The Campaign to Ban Landmines and the Landmine Ban Treaty," *Arizona Journal of International and Comparative Law*, Vol. 20, 2003, p. 589.

have agreed to a total ban on antipersonnel landmines.[27] Following this rapid success, the ICBL, along with its coordinator Jody Williams, received the 1997 Nobel Peace Prize.[28]

However, key world military powers, including the United States, China, and Russia, are not parties to the 1997 Ottawa Treaty, and retain stockpiles of antipersonnel mines and in some cases continue to deploy them. The U.S. government has been the subject of substantial pressure campaigns, including by retired military officials, to join the ban, but has resisted due to a desire to preserve an exception for the use of landmines in the Korean demilitarized zone (DMZ).[29] The refusal of these powerful states to join the Ottawa Treaty shows that the norm against the use of landmines has not been universally adopted, but it does not mean the norm has been ineffective, even in restraining the behavior of these same states. For example, in 2014 the United States codified a policy not to use antipersonnel landmines outside of the Korean DMZ, or to stockpile them for other uses, although this policy was later reversed under the Trump Administration.[30] China has ceased the export or sale of landmines and reduced much of its stockpile.[31] Russia, however, continues to actively use antipersonnel landmines, and the weapons have become a serious danger to civilians in the ongoing conflict in Eastern Ukraine.[32] The norm has therefore had some effects on even influential nonparties to the Ottawa Treaty, which have generally restricted their use of landmines in the face of

---

27 International Campaign to Ban Landmines, "Treaty Status," undated.

28 Nobel Prize, "The Nobel Peace Prize 1997," webpage, undated.

29 Wexler, 2003, pp. 577–578, 588; Vietnam Veterans of America Foundation, "An Open Letter to President Clinton," *New York Times*, April 3, 1996; and International Committee of the Red Cross, *Anti-Personnel Landmines: Friend or Foe? A Study of the Military Use and Effectiveness of Anti-Personnel Mines*, 1996.

30 White House, "Fact Sheet: Changes to U.S. Anti-Personnel Landmine Policy," September 23, 2014; U.S. Secretary of Defense, *DoD Policy on Landmines*, January 31, 2020.

31 Wexler, 2003, p. 592; Landmine and Cluster Munitions Monitor, *China: Mine Ban Policy*, September 24, 2019.

32 Landmine and Cluster Munitions Monitor, *Russian Federation: Mine Ban Policy*, December 18, 2019; Natalia Liubchenkova, "There's Only One Way to Tackle Ukraine's Infestation of Mines . . . Slowly," *Euronews*, March 13, 2019; and Maria Varenikova, "Battling Wildfire and Pandemic, Ukraine Faces a New Foe: Landmines," *New York Times*, October 3, 2020.

public and diplomatic pressure, but these effects have not been sufficient to restrict all use of landmines, and have had greater effects on the behavior of some of these states than others.

The rapid emergence of a norm against the use of landmines in the 1990s shows the potential effectiveness of efforts to use norms and related public and diplomatic pressure to change the military tools that states are willing to use. The strategies that the ICBL employed, including public information campaigns, a large coalition of NGOs with a centralized, simple message, and engagement with military leaders and experts, provide a potential roadmap for other efforts to build and establish norms restricting other state activities.

However, it is important to note that antipersonnel landmines have several characteristics that make them quite different from cyber capabilities, all of which would likely handicap the establishment of similar cyber norms. Landmines cause immediate, violent harm to civilians. Pictures of victims of landmine blasts, often missing limbs, were a regular feature of information campaigns around the necessity of the norm.[33] Advocates for the norm made a clear, simple case that all landmines should be banned, rather than a more complex, nuanced argument that they should be banned under certain circumstances that would have been more difficult to mobilize public opinion around.[34] Simply "banning" cyber capabilities on a blanket basis is obviously not feasible in the information age, meaning more nuanced (and therefore more difficult to explain) restrictions would likely be required. While the anti-landmine campaign therefore provides a relatively modern example of how public pressure and civil society can be mobilized to help build and establish a new norm restricting state capabilities, any similar efforts to attempt to restrict cyber capabilities would likely face a greater challenge.

Conclusion

This review of other types of international norms highlights several lessons for efforts to build norms in cyberspace, which will be

---

[33] Wexler, 2003, pp. 570–571.

[34] Carpenter, 2011, pp. 86–87; Wexler, 2003, p. 591.

incorporated into our proposals in Chapter Four. First, it shows that norms can affect state behavior even in circumstances where national leaders openly disagree with the content of those norms. Norms derive their ability to shape state behavior primarily from how they affect the expectations and behavior of the broader international or domestic societies in which states operate. Individual leader belief in the rightness of a given norm can of course be helpful in promoting or strengthening a norm, but it is not required. Given the current widespread disagreements among major states over key issues in cyberspace, as will be discussed in Chapter Three, norms have the potential to obviate the need to reach negotiated consensus while still imposing at least some restrictions on state behavior.

Second, this review highlights how norms can become established through "bottom-up" efforts, through the work of experts, NGOs, and civil society more broadly, rather than being negotiated or imposed by governments themselves. In areas where governmental consensus may be elusive, as is currently the case with respect to cyberspace, this history highlights potential alternative pathways for norms to become established.

Third, this review highlights something essential about the nature of successful norms. As successful norms require adoption and support from a wide range of individuals and actors, well beyond expert communities, if they are to be effective, they tend to be simple rather than complex, emotive rather than dry, and framed around avoiding risk to innocent life rather than around more abstract considerations. All these characteristics, however, pose substantial challenges to developing effective norms to govern behavior in cyberspace. Many types of behavior that policymakers may wish to prohibit or restrain in the cyber domain to promote stability can be highly technical in nature and may be difficult to observe or may have no immediate negative effects on human beings. One would expect mass mobilization of international or domestic public opinion to decry transgressions of such abstract norms to be quite difficult. Scoping and framing proposed cyber norms to incorporate these lessons and become more politically salient is likely to be a key element in determining their success.

CHAPTER THREE

The Current Status of International Dialogues on Cyber Norms

The effort to build norms in the cyber realm has been underway for several years, in both intergovernmental and private forums. These processes have already generated important lessons about the potential for such norms and about the gaps between the perspectives of major actors. In order to understand the potential for new norms in the cyber realm, in this chapter we first assess how cyber policies fit within the larger strategies of the major powers. We then review the status of existing dialogues and the implications they hold for future efforts.[1]

This survey of the current state of the cyber norm process reveals two main patterns, both of which pose significant hurdles to new progress. First, the three main cyber actors—the United States, Russia, and China—have starkly different priorities and perspectives on cyber issues and are nowhere near a level of consensus required for formalized agreement. And second, the process of intergovernmental, nongovernmental, and private-sector discussion of cyber norms has created a tangled thicket of manifestos, draft agreements, suggested principles, and other options for normative agreement. These realities appear to call into question the feasibility of the approach of seeking unified treaties or compacts as the primary means by which cyber competition might be restrained. Yet as Chapter Two suggests, such grassroots dialogues

1 An additional resource that very helpfully compiles and summarizes international statements and agreements that are related to the development of cyber norms is Carnegie Endowment for International Peace, "Cyber Norms Index and Timeline," webpage, last updated January 2021.

and proposals can also play a critical role in promoting the medium-term emergence of more enduring or established norms—a theme to which we return in the concluding chapter.

Major Power Perspectives on Cyber Norms

To identify potential next steps in developing cyber norms that may be fruitful, one key area of background to establish is how activities in cyberspace fit into the overall strategies of the key states involved: China, Russia, and the United States.[2] These states all view the cyber realm through somewhat different lenses, and their perspectives greatly constrain the types of agreements they are likely to support and the norms they would be willing to actively promote.

There are at least two areas where these three states are comparatively similar in their perspectives, if not their capabilities. The first is in the military or strategic domain. China, Russia, and the United States are all actively exploring how cyber capabilities could help to shape future battlefields, including by limiting the communications and awareness of adversaries, and disrupting the functioning of sophisticated weapons systems that rely on information technology.[3] All major powers are likely to retain an interest in developing and improving such capabilities, as well

---

[2] In choosing to focus on these three countries in our analysis, we considered both their overall cyber and technical capabilities as well as the broader national resources each state could potentially bring to bear on cyber issues, and their relevance for broader U.S. foreign policy challenges. That is, we focused on the cyber powers of greatest relevance for broader U.S. national security concerns. It is important to note, however, that a number of states may be relatively significant or comparable in their capabilities. A 2020 ranking of cyber power from the Belfer Center, for example, ranks the United States, China, and Russia first, second, and fourth, respectively, with the United Kingdom ranking third, and a number of other U.S. allies relatively close behind. See Julia Voo, Irfan Hemani, Simon Jones, Winnona DeSombre, Dan Cassidy, and Anina Schwarzenbach, *National Cyber Power Index 2020*, Belfer Center for Science and International Affairs, September 2020.

[3] For context, see Isaac R. Porche III, Christopher Paul, Chad C. Serena, Colin P. Clarke, Erin-Elizabeth Johnson, and Drew Herrick, *Tactical Cyber: Building a Strategy for Cyber Support to Corps and Below*, Santa Monica, Calif.: RAND Corporation, RR-1600-A, 2017; Elsa B. Kania and John K. Costello, "The Strategic Support Force and the Future of Chinese Information Operations," *Cyber Defense Review*, Vol. 3, No. 1, 2018; and Aaron Brantly and Liam Collins, "A Bear of a Problem: Russian Special Forces Perfecting Their Cyber Capabilities," Association of the United States Army, November 28, 2018.

as building resilience against their effects when used by others, particularly given the extreme difficulties in verifying any promises of disarmament in this area. The second area concerns their worry over the risks of cyber attacks on critical infrastructure such as power grids or hospitals. While the United States might be comparatively more exposed to such risks, as discussed below, this does represent a common area of vulnerability for all three states. In other areas, however, the strategic incentives of these states in cyberspace differ substantially.

For China, activities in cyberspace touch on at least two core strategic interests. First, China maintains an extensive series of controls over the content of domestic information networks, the so-called Great Firewall.[4] The Chinese Communist Party (CCP) is firmly committed to maintaining total control over content available to domestic internet users, including extensive monitoring and censorship, as well as restrictions on access to information from sources in other countries. This domestic control over the information environment is seen as vital to the CCP's hold on power, and the possibility that the control could be lessened represents a serious potential vulnerability for China. Beijing is highly unlikely to acquiesce to any international pressures to substantially weaken these internal controls, indeed preferring to extend its information control internationally.[5]

Second, the domestic legitimacy of the CCP regime also depends in large part on the delivery of continued economic growth. For many years, one contributor to this growth has been the widespread, aggressive theft of intellectual property from private firms in other states.[6]

---

4 Elizabeth C. Economy, "The Great Firewall of China: Xi Jinping's Internet Shutdown," *The Guardian*, June 29, 2018. An earlier RAND report that described China's perspectives on cyber competition is Scott W. Harold, Martin C. Libicki, and Astrid Stuth Cevallos, *Getting to Yes with China in Cyberspace*, Santa Monica, Calif.: RAND Corporation, RR-1335-RC, 2016.

5 Samm Sacks, "Beijing Wants to Rewrite the Rules of the Internet," *The Atlantic*, June 18, 2018.

6 White House Office of Trade and Manufacturing Policy, *How China's Economic Aggression Threatens the Technologies and Intellectual Property of the United States and the World*, June 2018; and Yukon Huang and Jeremy Smith, "China's Record on Intellectual Property Rights Is Getting Better and Better," *Foreign Policy*, October 16, 2019. It is also worth noting that whatever its economic benefits to China, this activity may have limits in how much it can close the military capabilities gap between the two states. See Andrea Gilli and Mauro Gilli, "Why China Has Not Caught Up Yet: Military-Technological Superiority and the Limits of Imitation, Reverse Engineering, and Cyber Espionage," *International Security*, Vol. 43, No. 3, 2019, pp. 187–189.

Chinese internal innovation capacity has developed gradually, but China still relies heavily on the transfer of technology and innovation from other countries to continue to grow and modernize its economy. While much of this technology transfer occurs via legal, voluntary means through coproduction or investment agreements, other transfers do not, and rely instead on espionage, often enabled by cyber intrusions. U.S. concern over the scope and scale of these intrusions led to the 2015 agreement between China and the United States to restrict state-directed commercial espionage.[7] The existence of the 2015 agreement does suggest that China may be willing to accept at least some restrictions on this type of cyber activity should sufficient pressure be applied.[8] However, the apparent demise of the agreement during the Trump administration also highlights how the maintenance of such agreements may be dependent on broader geopolitical developments.[9]

Russia's key concerns about cyberspace activities are similar to China's concerns regarding regime stability, but Moscow acts on these concerns in different ways. For example, while Russia is similarly concerned regarding the vulnerability it faces due to the potential for the domestic information environment to lead to unrest, it has historically been less restrictive than China in regulating its internal information environment in practice.[10] More recently, however, Russia has begun to escalate its domestic controls, bring its restrictions closer to,

---

[7] Scott W. Harold, "The U.S.-China Cyber Agreement: A Good First Step," *Cipher Brief*, July 31, 2016; and Adam Segal, "The U.S.-China Cyber Espionage Deal One Year Later," Council on Foreign Relations, September 28, 2016.

[8] Jack Goldsmith, "What Explains the U.S.-China Cyber 'Agreement'?" Lawfare Blog, September 26, 2015; and Shane Harris, "Obama Stares Down China on Cyberspying," *Daily Beast*, September 25, 2015.

[9] David E. Sanger and Steven Lee Myers, "After a Hiatus, China Accelerates Cyberspying Efforts to Obtain U.S. Technology," *New York Times*, November 29, 2018; and Ben Buchanan and Robert D. Williams, "A Deepening U.S.-China Cybersecurity Dilemma," Lawfare Blog, October 24, 2018.

[10] Ezekiel Pfeifer, "Why Doesn't Russia Censor the Internet Like China?" Institute of Modern Russia, April 15, 2015; and Valentin Weber, "Why China's Internet Censorship Model Will Prevail over Russia's," Council on Foreign Relations Blog, December 12, 2017.

though still short of, the Chinese approach.[11] These differences in the domestic approach to the internet, however, should not be interpreted as reflecting a lesser concern in the Kremlin regarding regime stability. If anything, Moscow may be more concerned than Beijing regarding the prospects for Western-assisted antigovernment demonstrations and actions.[12] Its more limited control of the information domain likely reflects a combination of a greater desire to preserve the economic utility of the internet (given the much smaller number of Russian speakers as opposed to Chinese speakers, and the resulting weaker state of Russian domestic alternatives to popular Western technology firms, a fully isolated Russian intranet would be of comparatively less value), as well as potentially technical or resource constraints.[13]

Perhaps the greater area of divergence between Chinese and Russian activities in the cyber domain has to do with offensive information operations targeting other countries. Russia has engaged in a series of aggressive, well-documented efforts to interfere in the political systems of other countries, including most notably the 2016 U.S. presidential election, the 2017 French presidential election, and numerous aspects of recent British politics.[14] While China has engaged in several information operations targeting U.S. allies and other states in Asia, such as

---

[11] Human Rights Watch, "Russia: Growing Internet Isolation, Control, Censorship," webpage, June 18, 2020; and Oleg Matsnev, "Kremlin Moves Toward Control of Internet, Raising Censorship Fears," *New York Times*, April 11, 2019.

[12] Olga Oliker, Christopher S. Chivvis, Keith Crane, Olesya Tkacheva, and Scott Boston, *Russian Foreign Policy in Historical and Current Context: A Reassessment*, Santa Monica, Calif.: RAND Corporation, PE-144-A, 2015; and Benjamin Denison, "Where US Sees Democracy Promotion, Russia Sees Regime Change," Russia Matters, July 29, 2020.

[13] Pfeifer, 2015; and Emily Parker, "Russia Is Trying to Copy China's Approach to Internet Censorship," *Slate*, April 4, 2017.

[14] Robert S. Mueller III, *Report on the Investigation into Russian Interference in the 2016 Presidential Election*, U.S. Department of Justice, March 2019; Heather A. Conley and Jean-Baptiste Jeangène Vilmer, *Successfully Countering Russian Election Interference*, Center for Strategic and International Studies, June 21, 2018; and Mark Landler and Stephen Castle, "'No One' Protected British Democracy From Russia, U.K. Report Concludes," *New York Times*, July 21, 2020.

Australia and New Zealand, these attempts appear to have been comparatively more limited in their aims and scope.[15]

From Moscow's perspective, these information operations, conducted in large part though not entirely in the cyber domain, likely serve several functions, including attempting to coerce Western states into ending perceived political interference in Russia or in regimes friendly to Moscow, as well as broader efforts to alter Western policy and cohesiveness.[16] The destabilizing activities that Russia has conducted in the cyber systems of other countries over the past decade therefore have a mixture of defensive and offensive motivations, but they are all clearly linked to Russia's perceptions of its overall strategic situation and closely integrated with other elements of national power and efforts to achieve broader strategic goals.

The United States has adopted a very different approach to cyber space than its more authoritarian competitors, although this approach does also have both defensive and offensive elements. Washington is mindful of the fact that, given its highly developed technology sector and the increasing integration of internet technologies into U.S. economic and social life, the United States likely has substantial economic vulnerabilities to disruptive cyber attacks.[17] The 2018 U.S. National Cyber Strategy, for example, makes the protection of U.S. cyber infrastructure and information systems the first of its four pillars.[18] This high level of potential vulnerability gives the United States a strong

---

[15] Amy Searight, "Countering China's Influence Operations: Lessons from Australia," Center for Strategic and International Studies, May 8, 2020; and Philip Crowe, "Will a Big Election Win for Ardern Reshape New Zealand's China Policy?" *World Politics Review*, October 1, 2020.

[16] Samuel Charap, "Strategic Sderzhivanie: Understanding Contemporary Russian Approaches to 'Deterrence,'" *Security Insights*, No. 62, September 2020; and Sarah Kreps, "The Shifting Chessboard of International Influence Operations," Brookings Institution, September 22, 2020.

[17] David C. Gompert, Astrid Stuth Cevallos, and Cristina L. Garafola, *War with China: Thinking Through the Unthinkable*, Santa Monica, Calif.: RAND Corporation, RR-1140-A, 2016, pp. 48–50; and Jack Goldsmith and Stuart Russell, *Strengths Become Vulnerabilities: How a Digital World Disadvantages the United States in Its International Relations*, Hoover Institution, Aegis Series Paper 1806, 2018.

[18] White House, *National Cyber Strategy of the United States*, September 2018.

incentive to dissuade potential adversaries from targeting the economic and technological infrastructure.

While the United States has expressed concern over external interference in the information domain, particularly as it affects U.S. domestic politics, this concern does not translate into any substantive desire to restrict the free and open nature of the U.S. domestic internet, as it has in both Russia and China. Instead, the United States has remained committed to the continued domestic and international openness of the internet. This desire to promote continued international openness reflects both commercial incentives, given the outsized role that U.S. technology companies play in the industry, as well as political, normative, and strategic commitments to continuing to promote freedom of expression and information.[19] Even though all three states share some concerns regarding domestic vulnerabilities in the information domain, it is this U.S. position that contrasts most sharply with the interests and positions of Russia and China with respect to the governance of cyberspace. More recently, the United States has also adopted a more aggressive offensive cyber policy, with the stated goal of deterring potential attacks on U.S. systems, in its "defend forward" approach.[20] Adopted in late 2018 by the Trump administration, as of this writing the fate of this approach in the new Biden administration remains to be seen. The potential implications of the "defend forward" program are discussed in greater detail in Chapter Four.

This brief summary has examined the essential perspectives of the three main cyber actors—the United States, China, and Russia. Significant differences of opinion exist among U.S. allies as well, and this discussion is not meant to imply that all allied or democratic countries share identical perspectives on information security or potential cyber norms. Many European countries, for example, have led the global effort to enhance the security of consumers' data and imposed

---

[19] Julie Makinen, "Chinese Censorship Costing U.S. Tech Firms Billions in Revenue," *Los Angeles Times*, September 22, 2015; J. S. Tan, "Big Tech Embraces New Cold War Nationalism," *Foreign Policy*, August 27, 2020; White House, 2018, pp. 24–26; and Shawn M. Powers, and Michael Jablonski, *The Real Cyber War: The Political Economy of Internet Freedom*, Champaign: University of Illinois Press, 2015.

[20] White House, 2018.

requirements on U.S. social media and search engine platforms that are distinct from those in the United States. Nonetheless, in terms of baseline cybersecurity and cyber stability goals, the United States and its primary democratic friends and allies do share a sufficient number of core concerns and have in the past endorsed enough overlapping ideas and proposals to support an important if not totally comprehensive agenda on cyber norms. In developing the proposals offered in Chapter Four, for example, we employed as one of our criteria building on ideas already approved in multilateral forums.

To summarize, the vastly different views and starkly different priorities regarding cyberspace and information operations between the United States on the one hand and Russia and China on the other—as well as the complex array of other actors in this space—would be expected to obstruct any easy consensus regarding cyber norms and acceptable activities in cyberspace. Different strategic perspectives of the threats from open versus closed information systems epitomize the gulf in attitudes, but these differences extend to smaller issues as well. China, for example, views the U.S. indictment of People's Liberation Army officers involved in hacking as a public affront and a violation of international law.[21] One would therefore expect progress in reaching agreement on what behaviors are legitimate in cyberspace to be halting, and this does indeed appear to be reflected in the history of such efforts, detailed below. These clearly different perspectives do not, however, preclude the potential for progress given the vulnerabilities, albeit of different types, that the major cyber powers do share. Potential ways forward are discussed in Chapter Four.

The Intergovernmental Dialogue

In 1999, the United Nations (U.N.) General Assembly passed the first resolution on the issue of what in the U.N. context is often referred to as information and communication technologies (ICTs). The resolution, proposed by the Russian Federation, called on member states to

---

[21] Harold, Libicki, and Cevallos, 2016, pp. 56–57; on China's general perspectives and how they differ from those of the United States, see pp. 17–35.

consider "existing and potential threats in the field" of ICTs that could "adversely affect the security of states."[22] The resolution invited states to share views on the development of international principles to improve ICT security and "combat information terrorism and criminality."[23] Russia's eventual goal was to turn the 1999 resolution into a new international treaty, but as the world of ICT evolved, consensus on ICT security became more difficult to achieve.

The 2010–2017 Group of Governmental Experts Process

In 2004, the U.N. formed GGE to discuss the formal development of international cyber norms and practices. The meeting concluded without consensus, and another meeting of the GGE was scheduled for 2010. This 2010 meeting would prove to be the first in a series of GGE meetings from 2010 to 2021.

2010 Group of Governmental Experts

In the years leading up to the 2010 GGE, international cyber attacks had risen significantly. These incidents included the widespread attack on Estonian organizations in 2007 and the 2008 breach of the U.S. military network, the latter of which led to the creation of the U.S. Cyber Command.[24] The increase in the destructive nature of cyber attacks highlighted the importance of ICT security in the international sphere. Yet the 2010 GGE did not result in any landmark resolutions, instead concluding with the consensus that there was a "lack of shared understanding regarding international norms pertaining to State use of ICTs," and that further dialogue was necessary to avoid misunderstandings and misperception between nations.[25]

---

[22] United Nations General Assembly, *Developments in the Field of Information and Telecommunications in the Context of International Security*, 53/70 A/RES/53/70 §, 1999.

[23] Jennifer Cheeseman Day, Alex Janus, and Jessica Davis, *Computer and Internet Use in the United States: 2003*, Special Studies, Current Population Reports, U.S. Census Bureau, October 2005.

[24] William J. Lynn III, "Defending a New Domain," *Foreign Affairs*, May 30, 2014.

[25] United Nations General Assembly, *Group of Governmental Experts on Developments in the Field of Information and Telecommunications in the Context of International Security*, A/65/201 §, 2010.

Following the 2010 GGE, Russia, China, Tajikistan, and Uzbekistan submitted a draft International Code of Conduct for Information Security to the U.N. in September 2011. The document declared that states would "lead all elements of society, including its information and communication private sectors, to understand their roles and responsibilities with regard to information security."[26] This clause was met with opposition by the United States, whose delegation stated that the inclusion of the clause would "legitimize the view that the right to freedom of expression can be limited by national laws and cultural proclivities, thereby undermining that right as described in the Universal Declaration on Human Rights."[27] The U.S. representative further stated that the draft code replaced existing laws with ambiguous concepts. Due to similar opposition from other nations, the proposal was not adopted.

In 2012, the World Conference on International Telecommunications (WCIT) was held in order to revise the U.N.'s 1988 International Telecommunications Union (ITU) treaty that standardized "global interconnection and interoperability" for everyday international telecommunication use, such as telephone calls.[28] During the negotiations, leaked documents implied that Russian president Vladimir Putin was looking to establish state-level control over the internet using the International Telecommunications Regulations (ITRs) treaty.[29] While the language of the final draft of the WCIT treaty was not as explicit in its approach to internet monitoring, it did state that "all governments should have an equal role and responsibility for international Internet

[26] United Nations, "Letter Dated 12 September 2011 from the Permanent Representatives of China, the Russian Federation, Tajikistan, and Uzbekistan to the United Nations Addressed to the Secretary-General," September 14, 2011.

[27] U.S. Department of State, "U.S. Intervention at the World Conference on International Telecommunications," December 13, 2012.

[28] International Telecommunications Union, International Telecommunication Regulations, WATTC-88 §, 1989.

[29] Already in 2011, Putin had told the Secretary General of the ITU that one of Russia's goals was "establishing international control over the Internet using the monitoring and supervisory capabilities of the [ITU]." Government of the Russian Federation, "Prime Minister Vladimir Putin Meets with Secretary General of the International Telecommunications Union Hamadoun Toure," 2011.

governance and for ensuring the stability, security and continuity of the existing Internet and it future development."[30] While Russia and China signed the final WCIT treaty, the United States chose not to.

2013 Group of Governmental Experts and Bilateral Agreements

At the 2013 GGE, nations agreed for the first time that "international law, and in particular the Charter of the U.N., is applicable" in cyberspace.[31] This agreement was considered a landmark in international cyber discussions, as it was the first time Russia and China had publicly declared this stance. The resolution also left open the possibility of establishing further norms and laws over time while acknowledging the relevance of existing frameworks.

In 2013, several bilateral meetings were held to further the international discussion of cyber norms. The United States and Russia established a new bilateral working group focused on ICT threats. The group would utilize the Nuclear Risk Reduction Center to increase transparency and avoid miscommunication during cyber incidents. Additionally, the United States and China created a bilateral working group to discuss and combat cyber issues. However, in May 2014, the United States accused five Chinese military officials of hacking into U.S. company data. China's foreign ministry argued that the accusation was based on "fabricated fact" and announced that it would suspend participation in the bilateral cybersecurity working group, thus suspending U.S.-China ICT security cooperation.[32]

2015 Group of Governmental Experts and Further Bilateral Agreements

In January 2015, another draft of the International Code of Conduct for Information Security was submitted to the United Nations

---

[30] Quoted in Kristen Eichensehr, "International Cyber Governance: Engagement Without Agreement?" Just Security, February 2, 2015.

[31] United Nations General Assembly, *Group of Governmental Experts on Developments in the Field of Information and Telecommunications in the Context of International Security*, A/68/98 §, 2013.

[32] Eric Tucker, "US Charges Chinese Officials in Cyberspying Case," AP News, May 19, 2014.

by China, Kazakhstan, Kyrgyzstan, Russia, Tajikistan, and Uzbekistan. Both versions of the code discussed a "multilateral, transparent and democratic" governance of ICTs that would counter the multistakeholder approach to internet governance supported by the United States and other states. The newer draft omitted the importance of grounding norms in existing international law as well as the agreement to not "proliferate information weapons or related technologies," instead focusing on the equal rights of states and importance of internet governance.[33]

The new draft also included clauses stating that signatories would not use ICTs for acts that would infringe on international peace or the stability of other states. It affirmed that rights of an individual offline must be protected online, "including the right and freedom to seek, receive and impart information."[34] However, this clause included restrictions that the United States disagreed with: These rights were not guaranteed where they infringed on the respect, rights, or reputation of others; or for the protection of national security, public order, public health, or public morals. The code was met with opposition by the United States and others, and it was not adopted by the U.N. General Assembly.

In June 2015, despite the lack of agreement regarding the newest code, interstate cooperation increased further with that year's landmark GGE resolution. The resolution agreed on 11 international norms for conduct in the ICT space. These held that states should: cooperate against terrorist and criminal use of ICTs; not allow their territory to be used for wrongful acts using ICTs; protect human rights on the internet; not commit or support breaking international law using ICTs; protect their infrastructure from ICT attacks; respond to requests from other states whose ICTs were attacked; protect their supply chains to maintain ICT product confidence; prevent the proliferation of malicious ICT tools; report ICT vulnerabilities; not hinder information

---

33 CCDOE, "An Updated Draft of the Code of Conduct Distributed in the United Nations—What's New?" undated.

34 United Nations, "Letter Dated 9 January from the Permanent Representatives of China, Kazakhstan, Kyrgyzstan, the Russian Federation, Tajikistan, and Uzbekistan to the United Nations Addressed to the Secretary-General," January 9, 2015.

system emergency response teams; and encourage the private sector and citizens to improve security and ICT use. As significant as these principles were, no progress was made on the applicability of international law in the cyber realm, an issue that would cause a greater divide at the next GGE.

Following the trend of cooperation on the 2015 GGE resolution in September 2015, Chinese president Xi Jinping and American president Barack Obama released a joint statement that affirmed that both states were "committed to making common efforts to further identify and promote appropriate norms of state behavior in cyberspace within the international community."[35] The leaders also affirmed that neither state would "conduct or knowingly support cyber-enabled theft of intellectual property."[36] The two nations furthered their commitment to ICT cooperation in December 2015 when the United States and China held a joint dialogue discussing the importance of improving cooperation and the quality and speed of responses to issues regarding cyber crime. The nations agreed to the development of a hotline mechanism and to a set of guidelines on combating cyber crime, and agreed to hold a tabletop exercise. Subsequently, many bilateral and multilateral statements affirmed the 2015 GGE norms and the norms around theft of intellectual property (IP). For instance, in the 2015 Group of 20 (G20) summit, 20 countries (including Russia and China) affirmed the applicability of international law and the prohibition on theft of IP for commercial gain.[37]

2017 Group of Governmental Experts

Since 2010, each GGE had been able to make significant landmark advances in international consensus on ICT issues, but this pattern of cooperation came to an end at the closure of the 2017 GGE. The representatives were unable to come to a consensus regarding the identification of threats to information security and the application of rules

---

[35] White House, "Remarks by President Obama and President Xi of the People's Republic of China in Joint Press Conference," Office of the Press Secretary, September 25, 2015.

[36] White House, "Remarks by President Obama and President Xi," 2015.

[37] Group of 20, "G20 Leaders' Communiqué Agreed in Antalya," Antalya Summit, November 15–16, 2015.

and norms to address those threats. The main issue during the debate revolved around the decision over how international law should be applied to ICT usage. The United States argued that the laws of war should be applied to cyberconflict, and that therefore new guidelines were not necessary for cyberspace as the U.N. Charter already contains accepted guidelines that have stood the test of time. Instead, the United States wanted explicit information on the right to self-defense, international humanitarian law, and the use of countermeasures in the event of a cyber attack.

On the other hand, Russia argued that a new multilateral cyber arms-control treaty was necessary to address the unique nature of cyberspace. Both Russia and China argued that such a new treaty could help prevent cyber-based conflict, and therefore the rules the United States was advocating for would not be necessary as cyberwarfare would not occur. China further argued that the development of specific rules and countermeasures implied the militarization of cyberspace, an outcome that China greatly opposed. The United States countered that the effort to develop a new treaty would "walk back progress" of previous meetings. It called on the GGE to establish clear rules on how international law applies to the rights of self-defense, humanitarian law, and state responsibility. Further disagreements spread from the conflict between the U.S.-supported idea of keeping a free and open internet, and the Russia and China stance that focused on preserving what they termed "cyber sovereignty" to ensure regime stability through state-level control.

At the conclusion of the talks, the U.S. representative stated that she was disappointed that other states were unwilling to accept the applicability of international law because those representatives "believe their States are free to act in or through cyberspace to achieve their political ends with no limits or constraints on their actions. That is a dangerous and unsupportable view, and it is one that I unequivocally reject."[38] The 2017 GGE simply ended up calling on member states to

[38] Markoff, Michele G., "Explanation of Position at the Conclusion of the 2016–2017 UN Group of Governmental Experts (GGE) on Developments in the Field of Information and Telecommunications in the Context of International Security," U.S. Department of State, June 23, 2017.

be guided by the 2015 report and work on considering and addressing current threats to a peaceful cyberspace.[39]

The 2019–2021 Group of Governmental Experts Process

Between 2019 and 2021, the GGE conducted its latest series of meetings, culminating in the issuance of a report in May 2021. This session ended on a more positive note, with a report that, in the words of Michael Schmitt, "managed to resurrect"[40] the GGE process after the failure of the previous round.[41]

Perhaps the most notable and important thing about the 2019–2021 GGE was that it managed to issue a consensus report at all after the failure of the earlier round and general degree of hostility among the main three cyber actors. Most of the basic content in the 2021 report reaffirms either what was in the 2015 GGE report or elements in the 2021 OEWG report, though it does extend the definition of a few normative issues, such as the requirements for peaceful settlement of disputes in the information realm.[42] For the first time in the GGE process, the report formally linked international humanitarian law to cyber norms and restraint.

The 2021 GGE report reemphasizes the risks posed by information threats and reaffirms the call on all UN member states to seek security and stability in this realm. It calls out the potential value of norms that "reflect the expectations of the international community and set standards for responsible State behavior."[43] The report urges countries to share information and collaborate in mitigating potential

---

[39] See Elaine Korzak, "UN GGE on Cybersecurity: The End of an Era?" *The Diplomat*, July 31, 2017.

[40] Michael Schmitt, "The Sixth United Nations GGE and International Law in Cyberspace," Just Security, June 10, 2021.

[41] See also Michele Markoff, "Remarks to the UN Group of Governmental Experts on Advancing Responsible State Behavior in Cyberspace in the Context of International Security," United States Mission to the United States, March 28, 2021.

[42] The report is available at United Nations Group of Governmental Experts (UN GGE), "Report of the Group of Governmental Experts on Advancing Responsible State Behaviour in Cyberspace in the Context of International Security," May 28, 2021.

[43] UN GGE, "Report of the Group of Governmental Experts," pp. 4–5.

cyber threats. Its strongest statements focus on the leading area of normative consensus: "A State should not conduct or knowingly support ICT activity contrary to its obligations under international law that intentionally damages critical infrastructure or otherwise impairs the use and operation of critical infrastructure to provide services to the public."[44]

The results of this latest round of the GGE therefore represent a worthwhile building block in the emergent effort to strengthen cyber norms. This outcome was especially important because it breathed new life into a process that seemed moribund after 2017, and did so with a consensus statement. The U.S. representative strengthened this collective message by tipping her hat to the efforts of Russian and Chinese participants. The report does, however, also signal strict limits to the existing intergovernmental process on cyber norms. Nothing in the statement represents a binding commitment. The report reflects an unresolved debate over the meaning of sovereignty in the digital realm and the degree to which it is a binding rule in the information realm or merely a principle. The report also remains vague about the true meaning and extent, or even formal existence, of a concept of due diligence in the cyber realm.

A Second Intergovernmental Track: The Open-Ended Working Group

Following the lack of consensus at the 2017 GGE, a fissure emerged about the principles governing the future of multilateral ICT deliberations. Two approaches dominated the debate, one backed by the United States and the other by Russia and China.

Resolution 73/27, proposed by Russia, China, Iran, and 28 other states, proposed the creation of an open-ended working group (OEWG) on international cyber norms and rules. It called for the OEWG to meet in 2019 and discuss security in the ICT in a "more democratic, inclusive, and transparent" manner that acted "on a consensus basis."[45]

---

[44] UN GGE, "Report of the Group of Governmental Experts," p. 9.

[45] United Nations 73rd Session First Committee, "Developments in the Field of Information and Telecommunications in the Context of International Security," Resolution 73/27, October 29, 2018.

This was in response to the fact that previous GGEs operated with up to 25 experts from a selection of countries, whereas the OEWG allowed for participation by any and all states that wished to join in the proceedings. The United States argued that the norms imposed by the 73/27 resolution were unacceptable and the language too broad, while claiming that the resolution tabled by the United States built more appropriately on the foundations of the original GGE.

Resolution 73/37, proposed by the United States, Germany, the United Kingdom, and 33 other states, stated that a new GGE should be created to replace the old one and continue negotiations. This new GGE would be guided by the prior GGE reports from 2010, 2013, and 2015 while focusing on addressing threats in the ICT space. It requested a group of 25 governmental experts to meet beginning in 2019 and continue studying cooperative measures for existing and potential threats in information security, "including norms, rules, and principles of responsible behavior of States."[46] Russia argued that the process of repeating the original GGE was a waste of resources that would rehash what had already been agreed, and that the selective nature was favorable only to a narrow scope of Western-interest countries.

In 2018, both proposals passed the U.N. General Assembly by majority voice vote,[47] creating two parallel processes to further the discussion on ICT security. Many countries voted for both resolutions, and even though the United States and United Kingdom had voted against the proposal for an open-ended working group, they still agreed to participate in the upcoming OEWG meetings. Following the adoption of the dual groups, the United States reiterated its intention to focus on adherence to and implementation of international rules while protecting human rights in cyberspace.

Prior to the first meeting of the OEWG, China submitted a working paper that focused on current threats to ICT infrastructure. The paper highlighted the threats of fake news eroding trust, cyber attacks

---

[46] United Nations 73rd Session First Committee, "Advancing Responsible State Behaviour in Cyberspace in the Context of International Security," Resolution 73/37, October 18, 2018.

[47] The resolution tabled by the United States received 139 votes in favor and 11 against, and the resolution tabled by Russia and China received 109 votes in favor and 45 against.

to critical ICT infrastructure, and how some states are using cybersecurity issues politically to suppress other states' ICT. It argued that since states have sovereignty in cyberspace, each nation should have jurisdiction over ICT infrastructures, be able to manage their state and citizens' affairs, not undermine other states' stability, and promote equalizing internet resources for all states.[48] This paper highlighted once again the lingering disagreement of basic perspectives, in which China and Russia focused on establishing sovereignty and control over the ICT environment, whereas the United States sought to promote a free and open cyberspace.

During the first substantive meeting of the OEWG, many states, including Russia and China, verbally confirmed the applicability of international law to the ICT sphere, and a majority of states agreed that the 2015 GGE resolution should serve as the foundation for further cyber norm discussions. However, states diverged on the application of international humanitarian law (IHL) to ICT. China argued that military and civilian objects were indistinguishable in cyberspace and thus applying IHL to cyberspace would require further study before it could be implemented. The Chinese representative paraphrased Ronald Reagan's speech on nuclear war, arguing that "cyberwar cannot be won and must never be fought," and therefore installing sanctions and public attributions as a response to cyber attacks would lead to greater instability.[49] Russia argued that while international law applied in cyberspace, a new, legally binding international agreement would be necessary to make this connection formal. Despite these disagreements, most states agreed that the implementation of confidence-building measures (CBMs) should be the priority of OEWG discussions. These measures can in turn support the development of norms by easing tensions and aligning state behaviors.

The OEWG issued a report in March 2021. It concluded, among other things, that "all stakeholders have a responsibility to use ICTs in a manner that does not endanger peace and security" and that "volun-

---

[48] UN Office for Disarmament Affairs, "Developments in the Field of Information and Telecommunications in the Context of International Security," undated.

[49] Nele Achten, "New U.N. Debate on Cybersecurity in the Context of International Security," Lawfare Blog, September 30, 2019.

tary, non-binding norms of responsible State behavior can reduce risks to international peace, security and stability and play an important role in increasing predictability and reducing risks of misperceptions, thus contributing to the prevention of conflict." The report recommended that "states should not conduct or knowingly support ICT activity contrary to their obligations under international law that intentionally damages critical infrastructure or otherwise impairs the use and operation of critical infrastructure to provide services to the public." The significant overlap between the latest reports of the OEWG and the GGE appears to have helped partially bridge the gap between these two processes.

Paris Call for Trust and Security in Cyberspace

Another governmental proposal in the area of cyber norms emerged in 2018, with the French government's announcement of this initiative. It is a combined public-private set of commitments and is therefore not an intergovernmental process per se, but dozens of states have signed the accord: By December 2020, 79 states, 32 public authorities at other levels, 368 nongovernmental groups, and 680 private-sector companies had endorsed its principles.[50]

The Paris compact includes nine principles to maintain cyber peace and stability. These overlap with many proposed norms of the GGE process and other suggested normative frameworks for cyber peace and stability. They are as follows:

1. **Protect individuals and infrastructure.** Prevent and recover from malicious cyber activities that threaten or cause significant, indiscriminate, or systemic harm to individuals and critical infrastructure.
2. **Protect the internet.** Prevent activity that intentionally and substantially damages the general availability or integrity of the public core of the internet.
3. **Defend electoral processes.** Strengthen our capacity to prevent malign interference by foreign actors aimed at undermining electoral processes through malicious cyber activities.

---

[50] The current status is shown at Paris Call for Trust and Security in Cyberspace, homepage, November 12, 2018. The wording of the nine principles included below comes from the same source.

4. **Defend intellectual property.** Prevent ICT-enabled theft of intellectual property, including trade secrets or other confidential business information, with the intent of providing competitive advantages to companies or the commercial sector.
5. **Nonproliferation.** Develop ways to prevent the proliferation of malicious software and practices intended to cause harm.
6. **Lifecycle security.** Strengthen the security of digital processes, products, and services, throughout their life cycle and supply chain.
7. **Cyber hygiene.** Support efforts to strengthen an advanced cyber hygiene for all actors.
8. **No private hack-back.** Take steps to prevent nonstate actors, including the private sector, from hacking back, for their own purposes or those of other nonstate actors.[51]
9. **International norms.** Promote the widespread acceptance and implementation of international norms of responsible behavior as well as CBMs to limit tensions and promote the development of norms in cyberspace.

These represent a significant agenda of cybersecurity. Although principle nine is termed "International Norms," in fact, several other principles, if adopted by multiple governments and increasingly adopted as expected practice, would count as norms by the definitions we are using here.

Nongovernmental Dialogues and Proposals

In this section we discuss three main categories of proposals put forth by scholars, think tanks, and private companies: (1) international law application guides, (2) codes of conduct, and (3) creation of regulatory

[51] This is somewhat qualified in the Paris Call presentation of the norm, which adds, "The Cybersecurity Tech Accord signatories strongly supported the decision to include Principle 8 in the Paris Call, which rightly introduces a general prevention on hacking back for non-state actors. However, this is an area fraught with ambiguity, and they believe further elaboration is needed to set clear boundaries around intent, authority, and intrusiveness before government and private actors can implement it." Paris Call for Trust and Security in Cyberspace, 2018.

bodies. Additionally, the report touches on proposed norm alternatives. These varying approaches highlight the range of methods and concepts that exist within the cyber norm debate in the pursuit of a peaceful cyber environment.

The Application of International Law

As noted above, some proposals for dealing with the risk of cyber aggression focus on the application of aspects of existing international law to cyber capabilities and actions. Some assessments of this issue distinguish between "international norms that carry a legally binding obligation" and "international norms that act as points of reference for expected behaviour but are not subject to legal enforcement mechanisms (e.g. legally non-binding voluntary norms of behaviour)."[52] One of the earliest examples of such a law-based proposal was suggested by Michael Schmitt and predated the creation of the GGE. This work, referred to as the "Schmitt Analysis" by scholars, was first published in 1998 and focused heavily on the U.N. Charter Chapter VII, Article 2(4), which prohibits the use of force.

The Schmitt Analysis argues that cyber threats differ from traditional threats in three ways: the means by which an attack takes place, the target of the attack, and the result of the attack. Furthermore, the nature of cyber attacks makes defining them difficult due to both the lack of a physical border that is crossed and the lack of a clear coercive instrument that can be classified as a weapon. In order to address these complications, the Schmitt Analysis proposes six criteria to determine whether a computer network attack should be classified as a use of force. For an attack to be declared a use of force, the severity, immediacy, directness, invasiveness, measurability, and presumptive legitimacy of the attack must be determined.[53]

---

[52] Anna-Maria Osula and Henry Rõigas, "Introduction," in Osula and Rõigas, eds., *International Cyber Norms: Legal, Policy and Industry Perspectives*, Tallinn: NATO Cooperative Cyber Defence Centre of Excellence, 2016, 11.

[53] Michael N. Schmitt, "Computer Network Attack and the Use of Force in International Law: Thoughts on a Normative Framework Essays on the Laws of War and War Crimes Tribunals in Honor of Teleford Taylor," *Columbia Journal of Transnational Law*, Vol. 37, No. 3, 1998.

If the attack follows these criteria, then it is an armed attack, and responses can and should follow the U.N. Charter. To determine whether a state has the right to respond to an unclear computer network attack, the attack must be part of an overall armed attack, it must be irrevocable and unavoidable, and the response must take place at the last possible moment.[54]

Additionally, the appropriateness of the response is determined by whether it is a breach of peace and thus falls under the right to self-defense as per the U.N. Charter. In 2011, Schmitt updated his analysis, broadening his criteria for what accounts for an armed attack in cyber operations. In addition to his original six criteria, he offered a seventh condition regarding responsibility, arguing that the closer a state is to action, the more responsibility it has for that action.[55] Both versions of the Schmitt Analysis rely on the U.N. Charter for classifying and responding to a computer network attack while leaning heavily on an international law–based approach.

Another proposed application of international law, the Tallinn Manual, released a version 1.0 and refined 2.0 and drew from an international group of experts, directed by Michael Schmitt in 2013 and 2017. The Tallinn Manual was set to answer the questions posed by Harold Koh in a 2011 speech at USCYBERCOM, which called for the establishment of unanimous "rules" that ground cyber conduct to the law.[56] The manual lays out the legality of cyber operations with respect to the following issues: sovereignty; due diligence; jurisdiction; the law of international responsibility; "cyber operations not per se regulated"; international human rights; diplomatic and consular law; the law of the sea; aviation law; space law; international telecommunication law; peaceful settlements to disputes; rules of force; *jus ad bellum* (just cause of war); *jus in bello* (just conduct of war); and prohibition of interven-

---

[54] Schmitt, 1998.

[55] Michael N. Schmitt, "Cyber Operations and the Jud Ad Bellum Revisited Norman J. Shachot Symposium," *Villanova Law Review*, Vol. 56, No. 3, 2011.

[56] Harold Hongju Koh, "International Law Cyberspace," paper presented at CYBERCOM Inter-Agency Legal Conference, Ft. Meade, Md., 2012.

tion.[57] As stated in the manual, "It is important to remember that the Experts who participated in the Tallinn Manuals were committed to stating the law as it was and producing manuals that would be understood to be their own views and not those of states."[58]

The manual seeks to operate as a starting point to the debate and highlights disagreements between experts throughout. For example, while all experts agreed that the human right regarding privacy in cyberspace "encompasses the confidentiality of communications," they did not agree as to whether this applied to "algorithmic inspections by machines."[59] The interpretation and application of international law will continue to evolve as the technology changes, pushing the boundaries of scholars' definitions of what is legal in cyberspace.

Code of Conduct Proposals

In the absence of a legal consensus, many nonstate actors have sought to lay out a code of conduct for cyberspace, building lists of activities that are permissible or prohibited by states and nonstate actors and seeking to fill in the gaps left by existing laws. One of these gaps, noted by several academics, cites concerns that the law of armed conflict does not clearly extend to the protection of financial data. The scholars argue that confidence in the financial system is integral to the survival of a state. Therefore, they propose that states adopt a norm that prohibits cyber attacks from targeting financial systems, which are critical infrastructure.[60] In order to ensure that this norm is properly adopted, the authors recommend "anchoring" the norm in a G20 agreement, and complementing the agreement with state-level declarations of intent to ensure it is adhered to during cyber conflicts.

---

[57] Eric Talbot Jensen, "The Tallinn Manual 2.0: Highlights and Insights International Justice: Where We Stand, Where We Fall, and Where We Need to Be," *Georgetown Journal of International Law*, Vol. 48, No. 3, 2016.

[58] Jensen, 2016.

[59] Jensen, 2016.

[60] Tim Maurer, Ariel Levite, and George Perkovich, *Toward a Global Norm Against Manipulating the Integrity of Financial Data*, Carnegie Endowment for International Peace, March 27, 2017.

Private firms can also play a key role in shaping perceptions of appropriate behavior by which states should abide, particularly in the cyber realm, where much relevant technical expertise—and many key cyber targets in need of protection—resides in the private sector. The company Microsoft has proposed a code of conduct, titled the "Digital Geneva Convention," to prevent states from developing cyber weapons, running cyber operations, and therefore committing attacks in the first place. In 2014, the company released a series of norms that argued that states should: exclude ICTs from cyber warfare; report vulnerabilities; avoid developing and building cyber weapons; limit offensive cyber engagements; and assist the private sector in cyber attack detection, response, and recovery.[61]

The "Digital Geneva Convention" was expanded in 2016 after Microsoft met criticism for focusing solely on state responsibilities. In the updated report, Microsoft acknowledged that "norms are not just for governments," and in addition to "offensive" and "defensive" norms, there are "industry norms" that should focus on defense and incident-response teams that collaborate to maintain security.[62] The new report further states that Microsoft had built two sets of norms, the first was for nation-states and are focused on exercising restraint, nonproliferation, limited engagement, and refraining from abuse of private-sector capabilities. Comparably, the latter set of norms was for ICT companies, and discussed how companies must collaborate, proactively patch and disclose vulnerabilities, and not allow malicious actors to use company systems. Microsoft called for the two sets of norms to work together to "identify, prevent, detect, respond to, and recover from events in cyberspace."[63]

Following this announcement, Microsoft worked to expand its industry norms to other ICT companies, an effort that culminated

---

[61] Angela McKay, Paul Nicholas, Jan Neutze, and Kevin Sullivan, "International Cybersecurity Norms: Reducing Conflict in an Internet-Dependent World," Microsoft Corporation, 2014.

[62] Scott Charney, Erin English, Aaron Kleiner, Nemanja Malisevic, Angela McKay, Jan Neutze, and Paul Nicholas, *From Articulation to Implementation: Enabling Progress on Cybersecurity Norms*, Microsoft, white paper, June 2016.

[63] McKay et al. 2014.

in the Cybersecurity Tech Accord of 2018. The accord focuses on protecting customers and products from vulnerabilities, protecting against tampering, refusing government requests for cyber attacks against "innocent citizens and enterprises," empowering users to practice smart cybersecurity, and cooperating between companies.[64] This effort, signed by 34 companies, moved the norms discussion to the industry level and provided a baseline for how companies should be operating.[65]

Two years after the accord was first announced, it had 144 signatures from global technology firms, including industry giants such as Facebook, Nokia, Intuit, and Salesforce.[66] Notably, these signatories include Cisco, Dell Technologies, and NTT, which have also signed another cooperation-led code of conduct, the "Charter of Trust" written in 2018 and sighed at the Munich Security Conference. The charter outlines ten principles that call on governments, companies, schools, and other stakeholders to maintain confidence in technology through supply-chain protection, transparency, ownership, regulation, education, innovation, user- and security-focused design, and protection of critical infrastructure.[67] By proposing both government- and industry-level norms, corporations are positioning themselves to have a voice in the development of the concept of cybersecurity and permissible cyberspace actions.

The final notable code of conduct, proposed in 2018, echoes the same multidisciplinary approach as the charter by outlining principles for state and nonstate actors in one document, titled the "Norm Package Singapore." The package was written by the Global Commission on Stability of Cyberspace, built from the efforts of two European think tanks and funded by Microsoft, the Internet Society, and several coun-

---

[64] Cyber Tech Accord, "Cybersecurity Tech Accord," 2018.

[65] For analyses of Microsoft's process of developing itself as a norm entrepreneur, see Louise Marie Hurel and Luisa Cruz Lobato, "Unpacking Cyber Norms: Private Companies as Norm Entrepreneurs," *Journal of Cyber Policy*, Vol. 3, No. 1, 2018; Brenden Kuerbis and Farzaneh Badiei, "Mapping the Cybersecurity Institutional Landscape," *Digital Policy, Regulation and Governance*, Vol. 19, No. 6, 2017; and Tim Maurer, "Private Companies Take the Lead on Cyber Security," War on the Rocks, May 4, 2018.

[66] Cyber Tech Accord, "Cybersecurity Tech Accord Celebrates Its Second Anniversary," February 25, 2020.

[67] Other significant signatories include Allianz, Mitsubishi, and Deutsche Telekom.

tries, including France and Singapore. The writers acknowledged that their work was a culmination of norms identified by the United Nations GGE, the G20, the Group of 7, Microsoft, and other stakeholder groups.

The package outlines six norms covering antitampering, antibotnet, vulnerability disclosures, stability prioritization, cyber hygiene, and nonstate cyber pacifism.[68] These norms are unique in their combination of responsibly at all levels of the ICT chain, from various stakeholders and individual companies to multilateral state interactions. The proposals seek in part to fill in the gaps left by the GGE. Except for Microsoft's early proposals, all of the above occurred within two years, in 2017 and 2018. This shows a dramatic increase in interest in a code of conduct for the internet, and the cascading effect that declaring norms can have on the private sector.[69] The development of these codes of conduct by nonstate actors is worthy of significant attention as the cyber norm debate evolves, because noting what they prioritize in cyberspace will show which norms they are willing to adapt and enforce.

Norm Enforcement Regulatory Bodies

Some stakeholders have considered stronger methods of ensuring norm compliance than signing multiple accords, charters, and codes, instead subscribing to the idea of stronger control over cyber behavior by proposing the creation of regulatory bodies to preside over new cyber norms, with a more explicit focus on cooperative mechanisms to enhance information security. The company NTT, a proponent of both the accord and the charter described above, assisted in developing the initiative Mutually Agreed Norms for Routing Security (MANRS). This effort, which was first signed into existence in 2014 by Comcast,

---

[68] Global Commission on the Stability of Cyberspace, *Norm Package Singapore*, December 16, 2018.

[69] For discussions on company contributions to the cyber norm debate, see Amanda N. Craig, Scott J. Shackelford, and Janine S. Hiller, "Proactive Cybersecurity: A Comparative Industry and Regulatory Analysis," *American Business Law Journal*, Vol. 52, No. 4, 2015; and Maurer, 2018.

NTT, and Time Warner Cable, now has over 300 participants.[70] The goal of MANRS is to make both stakeholders and users more aware of existing security problems while promoting a culture of shared responsibility for internet access and routing security. MANRS focuses on industry-level compulsory and recommended actions for all participants to shore up security while routing internet traffic.[71] In addition to the actions of network operators, MANRS members are beholden to a set of "conformance requirements" that must be adhered to in order to gain and maintain eligibility in the group. An audit, which occurs when the operator joins MANRS and then on a spot-check basis, verifies that the operator is preventing incorrect routing, stopping spoofed traffic, and facilitating global communication and routing.[72] Through this process of compliance and accountability, MANRS seeks to create a group of norm adherents at the operational level.

Existing U.S. Policy and Practice

As noted above, the United States has undertaken significant internal discussions and international diplomacy around the issue of cyber norms. It issued a formal report titled *International Strategy for Cyberspace* in 2011,[73] began a more focused governmental process to build norms in about 2013, and first articulated its baseline set of proposed peacetime norms in 2014–2015. The U.S. national policy underlying its participation in these norm-development processes has reflected a relatively consistent strategic vision and set of proposals for almost a decade. As noted in a May 2020 speech by then Assistant Secretary of State Christopher Ford, that strategy involves an effort to build "an international

[70] Other notable signatories include Amazon, Google, Microsoft, and Netflix. See Kieren McCarthy, "Watch Your MANRS: Akamai, Amazon, Netflix, Microsoft, Google, and Pals Join Internet Routing Security Effort," *The Register*, 2020.

[71] MANRS.org, "Mutually Agreed Norms for Routing Security (MANRS)," September 20, 2019.

[72] MANRS.org, 2019.

[73] White House, *International Strategy for Cyberspace: Prosperity, Security, and Openness in a Networked World*, May 2011.

framework of responsible state behavior in cyberspace" and has three basic components:

1. the affirmation that existing international law applies to state behavior in cyberspace just as it does in other potential conflict arenas (i.e., that cyberspace is not a lawless, "anything goes" domain, even in wartime)
2. adherence to certain nonbinding norms of responsible state behavior in cyberspace during peacetime
3. the development and implementation of practical CBMs to reduce the risk of conflict and escalation in cyberspace.[74]

Codifying and promoting cyber norms in the United States will require navigating a complex interagency dynamic characterized by conflicting equities. For example, the U.S. Intelligence Community and the Department of Defense already engage in an array of cyber operations, seeing them as essential to their missions. For this reason, those agencies tend to prefer norms governing offensive cyber operations that ensure maximum freedom of action. In general, the U.S. government tends to have more appetite for norms focused on other types of destabilizing cyber activity in which it does not participate (for instance, ransomware), or for enforcement and cost-imposition actions that seek to support the development of existing norms in practice.

Many basic elements of the U.S. approach were laid out in the *International Strategy for Cyberspace*, released in May 2011 (and referenced above). This initial strategy outlined several broad principles of responsible state conduct that ought to govern normative constraints in cyberspace. These were

- **Upholding fundamental freedoms.** States must respect fundamental freedoms of expression and association, online as well as off.
- **Respect for property.** States should in their undertakings and through domestic laws respect intellectual property rights, including patents, trade secrets, trademarks, and copyrights.

[74] Christopher Ford, "Cyberspace Security Diplomacy: Deterring Aggression in Turing's Monument," remarks at the Foreign Service Institute, May 13, 2020.

- **Valuing privacy.** Individuals should be protected from arbitrary or unlawful state interference with their privacy when they use the internet.
- **Protection from crime.** States must identify and prosecute cyber criminals, ensure that laws and practices deny criminals safe havens, and cooperate with international criminal investigations in a timely manner.
- **Right of self-defense.** Consistent with the United Nations Charter, states have an inherent right to self-defense that may be triggered by certain aggressive acts in cyberspace.[75]

The strategy then added a number of principles to constrain state behavior, which it argued were more specific to the requirements of the information realm. These were

- **Global interoperability.** States should act within their authorities to help ensure the end-to-end interoperability of an internet accessible to all.
- **Network stability.** States should respect the free flow of information in national network configurations, ensuring that they do not arbitrarily interfere with internationally interconnected infrastructure.
- **Reliable access.** States should not arbitrarily deprive or disrupt individuals' access to the internet or other networked technologies.
- **Multistakeholder Governance.** Internet governance efforts must not be limited to governments, but should include all appropriate stakeholders.
- **Cybersecurity due diligence.** States should recognize and act on their responsibility to protect information infrastructures and secure national systems from damage or misuse.

These principles largely mirror the basic normative concepts embedded in intergovernmental processes like the GGE, in private-sector proposals like the Paris Initiative, and in many aspects of principles grounded in international law, like the Tallinn Manual. Some

---

[75] White House, 2011, p. 10.

version of these principles has governed the basic U.S. approach to this issue since 2011.

This consistency is evidenced in a 2015 speech by John Kerry in which he discussed the U.S. effort to build "a broad consensus on where to draw the line between responsible and irresponsible behavior." Kerry first stressed the established U.S. principle that "the basic rules of international law apply in cyberspace," meaning that "Acts of aggression are not permissible. And countries that are hurt by an attack have a right to respond in ways that are appropriate, proportional, and that minimize harm to innocent parties." He also listed the peacetime cyber norms the U.S. had proposed:

> First, no country should conduct or knowingly support online activity that intentionally damages or impedes the use of another country's critical infrastructure. Second, no country should seek either to prevent emergency teams from responding to a cybersecurity incident, or allow its own teams to cause harm. Third, no country should conduct or support cyber-enabled theft of intellectual property, trade secrets, or other confidential business information for commercial gain. Fourth, every country should mitigate malicious cyber activity emanating from its soil, and they should do so in a transparent, accountable and cooperative way. And fifth, every country should do what it can to help states that are victimized by a cyberattack.[76]

That same year, the United States contributed three leading proposals for GGE norms, which again drew on the basic principles laid out in 2011.[77] It proposed that participating states should not launch or support cyber attacks that either damage or impair critical infrastructure or obstruct responses to cyber emergencies, and that they cooperate with other countries in prosecuting cyber crime launched from their territory.

U.S. policy continues to reflect this overall emphasis on conscientious behavior in the digital realm and the same essential set of principles that represent such behavior. In an October 2020 speech, for

[76] John Kerry, "An Open and Secure Internet: We Must Have Both," remarks at Korea University, U.S. Department of State, May 18, 2015.

[77] Marks, 2015.

example, Assistant Secretary Ford noted that "one critical plank of the U.S. agenda is to promote clear understandings of what constitutes responsible State behavior in cyberspace." The initial foundation for the U.S. approach, he stressed, was gaining general agreement to the applicability of international law in cyberspace:

> One of these key principles is the idea that international humanitarian law, international human rights law, and indeed also the United Nations Charter itself, apply to State behavior in cyberspace in the event of armed conflict. Led by the United States, a broad coalition of diplomats carried the day on this at the 2013 cyber GGE, which articulated by consensus that "[i]nternational law, and in particular the Charter of the United Nations, is applicable and is essential to maintaining peace and stability and promoting an open, secure, peaceful[,] and accessible [cyberspace] environment." This conclusion was reiterated by a subsequent GGE in 2015, and both reports have been endorsed by U.N. Member States.[78]

One important component of the U.S. strategy to achieve these goals has been an effort to build a "big tent" coalition of states affirming these norms, including through a Cyber Deterrence Initiative of like-minded states that would impose costs on those that violate agreed-upon redlines.[79] It has engaged in dozens of high-level, whole-of-government, bilateral and multilateral cyber meetings with allies, partners, friends, and rivals since 2011. Some of these dialogues and engagements include participation with the private sector (for instance, the U.S.-India cyber dialogue, which has robust private-sector participation).

However, at least since the Snowden disclosures, many other states view the United States as refusing to live by the principles for responsible behavior that it has enunciated, undermining support for the norms the United States formally enunciates. Examples of cyber operations that international audiences often cite as violating proposed norms

---

[78] Christopher Ford, "Responding to Modern Cyber Threats with Diplomacy and Deterrence," Speech at the Center for Strategic and International Studies, October 19, 2020.

[79] Ford, "Responding to Modern Cyber Threats," 2020.

include the Stuxnet attack. Most recently, the Trump administration, in National Security Presidential Memorandum (NSPM)-13, loosened the restrictions on offensive cyber operations, and the United States has moved to more aggressively "defend forward" in cyberspace.[80]

Given its own behavior in the cyber realm, and in particular emerging doctrines of "active defense" and anticipatory disruption, the credibility of the United States as a leader of the effort to build cyber norms is in question. Other states, led by but not limited to Russia and China, find U.S. actions to be incompatible with U.S. pressure for universal adherence to its proposed cyber norms. The U.S. capacity for such operations, as part of a deterrent posture, can be an important counterpart to normative constraints in restraining adversary behavior. However, unilateral, sometimes offensive, and anticipatory self-defense measures can also inhibit or undermine the potential development of cyber norms.[81] As we will argue, signaling a willingness to restrain these activities—in ways that still leave the United States able to engage in necessary self-defense—will be critical to setting the stage for progress on norms.

Summary: The Current Status of Cyber Norm Proposals

While states all agree on the priority of information security and controlling cyber aggression, therefore, the existing intergovernmental process suggests that—notwithstanding the latest consensus report of the GGE—the agreement breaks down when the debate turns to specifics. This is compounded by the question of enforceability and verifiability in cyberspace. Right now, states are currently in a place where they are cherry-picking cyber norms and following only the rules they find convenient. Few observers believe that Russian or Chinese behav-

[80] Mark Pomerleau, "New Authorities Mean Lots of New Missions at Cyber Command," FifthDomain.com, May 8, 2019; and Erica D. Borghard and Shawn W. Lonergan, "To Defend Forward, the U.S. Must Strengthen the Cyber Mission Force," Lawfare Blog, March 13, 2020.

[81] The Cyberspace Solarium Commission notably recommended updating the National Cyber Strategy to clarify how "defending forward" can be integrated into other aspects of U.S. strategy in cyberspace. U.S. Cyberspace Solarium Commission, 2020, p. 2.

ior in this realm will be significantly constrained by the aspirations of existing intergovernmental statements or processes.

At this point, it does not appear likely that one fundamental issue under dispute—the claim of autocratic regimes like China and Russia of a right to control their "information borders" in a form of cyber sovereignty—can be resolved through negotiation. The United States and many other countries support a principle of access to information, but such an agreement could not be part of any collection of agreed cyber principles at this point. For the time being, the United States may need to postpone a negotiated resolution and consider other ways forward.[82]

This current status of international discussions therefore does not provide the basis for believing that any large-scale agreements on cyber norms, beyond the aspirational statements accumulating in several intergovernmental processes, are feasible in the near term. This is true in part because of the fundamental divergence in perspectives between the United States on the one hand and China and Russia on the other: the United States favors a globally open internet and exchange of information. It has been unwilling to consider constraints on what most U.S. officials believe to be legitimate democracy-promotion efforts or wider information transmission, things that Russia and China seek to constrain in proposals for cyber norms. Russia and China place a high premium on "cyber sovereignty" and control of information flows. This divergence is unlikely to be resolved in the short term, and efforts to create normative constraints on cyber aggression must work around that fact.

One implication is that the recurrent Russian proposal to reach a general treaty constraining such activities, perhaps grounded in international law, is likely not in the cards. The perspectives of major powers are simply not well enough aligned to support such a treaty, and the negotiations over one are likely to become bogged down in debates that return to fundamental differences in perspective. There is limited room for overlap in preferences to produce a voluntary agreement or

---

[82] Eneken Tikk and Mika Kerttunen, *The Alleged Demise of the UN GGE: An Autopsy and Eulogy*, New York: Cyber Policy Institute, 2017, pp. 17–18.

treaty in which the parties would mutually agree to restrain themselves on all key issues.

Indeed, given the existing U.S. efforts and clear barriers to new progress, as well as the failure of recent U.S. pressure on Russian and Chinese cyber malfeasance (through indictments, sanctions, and other means), the Biden administration has to define carefully and narrowly what it is trying to achieve and how it aims to do so in this field.

This analysis suggests that rather than a top-down, "inside-out" option built around a formalized agreement among the major cyber powers, the United States may have more success with a more bottom-up, "outside-in" strategy of building gradual momentum for norms that it perceives to be most essential—an approach that has also been part of U.S. practice since roughly 2011.[83] Such an approach would begin with an effort to establish a set of clear principles that the United States believes should be "beyond the pale" in cyberspace, and then would use diplomacy, support for nongovernmental processes, and collaboration with NGOs, private companies, and like-minded states to gain widespread international and public support for those as norms. These steps would increase public and diplomatic pressure on Russia and China to comply by shifting their calculations of the benefits and costs of engaging in destabilizing behavior in cyberspace. Chapter Four outlines several possible components of such a strategy.

---

[83] See, for example, the explicit discussion of normative as opposed to formal arms-control constraints in Christopher Ford, "Rules, Norms, and Community: Arms Control Discourses in a Changing World," European Union Council on Nonproliferation, December 14, 2019.

CHAPTER FOUR

Identifying Next Steps in Cyber Norm Development

Based on the analysis of the character of norms, the history of cyber norm development, U.S. positions and practices, Russian and Chinese perspectives and goals, and other issues, we assessed potential next steps for U.S. policy designed to build norms in this area. This chapter examines several challenges, constraints, and opportunities relevant to the task of developing a U.S. cyber norm agenda and concludes with specific recommendations.

Any renewed U.S. commitment to the development of normative constraints in the cyber realm must take seriously three important facts that set the context for this issue—and in ways that generate real constraints on a new cyber norms agenda. First, developing norms to regulate state conduct in the information realm must be viewed as only one part of an integrated strategy for safeguarding U.S. information security. Given the stakes, such an overarching strategy should be wide-ranging and comprehensive, a new NSC-68 for the digital era—a national-level grand strategy designed to preserve national security.[1] International cyber norms can support other elements of a comprehensive strategy but need not solve every problem on their own. Norms themselves, for example, are usually silent about the deterrent policies states would adopt to punish violations of those norms.[2]

---

1 We are indebted to Alex Klimburg for this comparison.

2 For one recent argument about aggressive cyber deterrence policies, see Emily O. Goldman, "From Reaction to Action: Adopting a Competitive Posture in Cyber Diplomacy," *Texas National Security Review*, Fall 2020.

An overarching U.S. strategy for information security should have several primary elements.[3] As the U.S. Cyberspace Solarium Commission suggested, such a strategy will certainly have to include comprehensive, layered efforts to promote resilience and deterrence. It will necessarily incorporate programs and policies to enhance domestic information-security resilience and the security of domestic election systems. In terms of rules and norms, any U.S. strategy will have to address the challenge of promoting international technical standards that improve the global security of the internet; assist the private sector and NGOs; enhance processes and conventions to promote transparency; share best practices, tools, and techniques; engage in naming and shaming of norm violators; and support capacity-building programs to enhance the information-security capabilities of other countries. Such initiatives could incorporate some role for international law, though relying solely on legal prohibitions on armed attack is unlikely to be effective. Any U.S. strategy in cyberspace must reserve a major role for deterrent policies and capabilities for responses in kind, in terms of both unilateral and multilateral efforts at detection, response and punishment.

These various elements of a response should be viewed as complementary to one another, and not either-or choices. Each plays a critical role in the larger effort. In particular, the role of unilateral means of self-defense is especially important as a complement to normative agreements. Indeed, in some ways, norms should be properly viewed as a way of building a framework within which self-defense can be made more effective.

Michael P. Fischerkeller and Richard J. Harknett, for example, have argued for a form of "agreed competition" that allows for significant offensive cyber espionage and even disruptive activities on the assumption that this realm is not suitable for outright deterrence of aggressive actions.[4] They contend that sustained engagement, including some degree

---

[3] Some of these elements are drawn from Global Commission on the Stability of Cyberspace, 2019, p. 14. An excellent summary of components of a cybersecurity regime is Alexander Klimburg, ed., *National Cybersecurity Framework Manual*, Tallinn: NATO Cooperative Cyber Defence Centre of Excellence, 2012.

[4] Michael P. Fischerkeller and Richard J. Harknett, *Persistent Engagement, Agreed Competition, Cyberspace Interaction Dynamics, and Escalation*, Institute for Defense Analyses, May 2018.

of offensive operations, in the cyber realm will not trade off against norm development; it will help lay the groundwork for such development. "If the United States is to shape the development of international cyberspace norms that will bring stability and security," they suggest elsewhere, "it can do so primarily through strategic cyber campaigns that begin to shape directly and indirectly the parameters of responsible behavior."[5] The precise balance of operational engagement and norm development in U.S. policy is beyond the scope of this essay, but we agree that these various elements of U.S. policy must be designed to work together to produce the best possible incentives for cyber stability and restraint.

We do not therefore envision the process of norm development outlined in this report as sufficient, in and of itself, to either protect U.S. interests in the information domain or to create enforceable global rules against certain forms of cyber aggression. As in all areas of U.S. national security strategy, norms are designed to supplement and enhance the effectiveness of unilateral means of self-defense, including resilience and deterrence. But in the cyber realm in particular, the limitations on effective self-defense mean that those unilateral steps will be far more likely to work if undertaken in the context of increasingly accepted normative constraints on state behavior.

A second critical piece of the context for cyber norm development is the simple fact that the process of debating and developing such norms has now been underway for roughly 20 years. It began at least with the GGE process in the early 2000s, but even that built on earlier proposals for the role of international law stretching back to the 1990s. The U.S. program for promoting and catalyzing norms has been active since at least 2011, with the release of the U.S. cybersecurity strategy. Efforts at norm development have proceeded internationally through dozens of multilateral meetings and forums and a series of high-level bilateral dialogues, the latest of which produced an important consensus report in May 2021. The U.S. Department of State now has an extensive track record in cyber diplomacy, and Congress has been urging the department to formalize these efforts in a dedicated bureau.

[5] Michael P. Fischerkeller and Richard J. Harknett, "Deterrence Is Not a Credible Strategy for Cyberspace (and What Is)," Institute for Defense Analysis, 2017, p. 3.

There is also an accumulating history of state practice in terms of cyber restraint.[6] States with potent cyber capabilities have yet to unleash anything close to the full capabilities they possess or seek to do catastrophic damage to other societies. We also observe instances of states retreating from more aggressive behavior when confronted with potential costs. China, for example, stepped back from the intensity of its cyber-enabled intellectual property theft when confronted by the United States in 2015. This evidence suggests that states do weigh the risks and costs of cyber manipulation and aggression. Norms can contribute to this process by adding to the potential reputational or material costs of cyber aggression that violates their standards.

In other words, the process of norm emergence we described in Chapter Two has begun. The U.S. task now is not simply to begin it or take it seriously, but rather to identify the next steps that would have the most lasting effect in advancing that process, and to shape its development in directions that are most likely to advance U.S. interests.

Third and finally, however, any new U.S. strategy must contend with the very real, and sometimes crippling, differences among major states in both the goals and tactics of the process of cyber norm development. The United States, Russia, and China have fundamental disagreements about free access to online information and the meaning of cyber sovereignty, among other issues. Any new effort must take seriously these barriers to practical effect. Making progress will not be as simple as undertaking new initiatives or putting more effort into these goals. There may be practical limits to what can be achieved in the near term, and a U.S strategy must include components that have value even without major breakthroughs.

To outline what such a strategy might look like, this chapter first outlines the possible goals of a regime of cyber norms. It then examines the role of state practice in promoting norm development, and describes the essential strategic concept of the proposed approach to cyber norms—one that is both *catalytic* and *multistakeholder*. The

---

[6] Jason Healey and Robert Jervis, "The Escalation Inversion and Other Oddities of Situational Cyber Stability," *Texas National Security Review*, Fall 2020.

chapter then proposes criteria for assessing the effectiveness of cyber norms, and outlines an agenda for U.S. policy on cyber norms over the next several years that operates within the opportunities and constraints offered by the three contextual factors noted above.

Objectives of a Normative Regime

U.S. goals in promoting a normative regime governing cyber aggression should guide the approach to achieving them. To identify appropriate and desirable U.S. goals, however, requires first understanding how dynamics in cyberspace overlap with two much larger policy issues. One is the degree of intensity of the U.S. strategic competition with Russia and China, and the degree to which the United States seeks—or those countries perceive that it is seeking—the disruption of the current ruling regimes in Moscow and Beijing. Russia and China both emphasize the importance of state sovereignty and place a high priority on controlling outside interference. The United States has broader policy choices to make about how to handle that issue, choices that will have implications for the character of the cyber norms it would be willing to endorse.

The second wider policy issue is even more fundamental: shaping the future information environment to preserve, rather than undermine, democratic societies. Addressing this issue will require difficult decisions for U.S. policymakers—for example, about the degree of regulation or oversight of social media platforms—that touch on core elements of U.S. domestic society.

Broader U.S. strategies on these two core issues will directly inform the objectives of U.S. policy with respect to cyber norms. For example, one of the critical questions regarding objectives involves the distinction between political interference—the current focus of much U.S. concern—and wider cyber-enabled aggression. Some proposals would pursue concepts designed to radically reduce foreign interference in social media platforms intended to reach American audiences, which is of course much broader than a narrower focus on cyber attacks against, for example, election infrastructure.

A related question is what specific purposes a cyber norms regime would have relative to other national efforts. For example, in terms of political interference, the United States could impose and enforce new prohibitions on the hosting of foreign broadcast entities in the United States, place new requirements on social media platforms to control the use of automatically generated messaging and to remove messages with extremist themes, and other steps. The United States can take these and other unilateral steps to improve the security of its electoral systems.[7] But they will need to be considered alongside the cyber norms the United States is seeking to promote more broadly and the international actions the United States undertakes in cyberspace.

We can also distinguish cyber norms, and the objectives they seek, from the establishment of information-security procedures, coordination efforts, and standards. Basic technical propositions about cybersecurity, many promulgated by private-sector coalitions, can define tools and means for pursuing information-security goals. A normative regime is designed to generate higher-level principles for state conduct. Some suggestions appearing on lists of cyber "norms" are really more fundamental statements about the need for collaboration on information-security standards.

These considerations suggest that the goals of U.S.-promoted cyber norms will likely not include preventing any foreign influence operations, but instead placing guardrails around any specific form of cyber attack that "destabilizes the fragile equilibrium" of U.S. relations with its two main competitors, Russia and China.[8] Eventually, the United States may seek to develop more specific norms that regulate narrower forms of cyber aggression. For now, however, the most urgent need is to create broad constraints that keep information-based conflict from metastasizing and creating highly unstable dynamics among major powers. For example, foreign cyber operations that led to genuine uncertainty regarding the outcome of national elections or

---

7 See Kim Zetter, "Fixing Democracy: The Election Security Crisis and Solutions for Mending It," *Texas National Security Review*, Fall 2020.

8 Bruce McConnell, Pavel Sharikov, and Maria Smekalova, "Suggestions on Russia-U.S. Cooperation in Cybersecurity," Russian International Affairs Council and East-West Institute, Policy Brief No. 11, May 2017, p. 7.

substantial deaths or economic losses could result not only in domestic instability but also in a perceived need to respond in escalatory terms against the responsible state.

In the cyber realm, unlike areas of major military capabilities, threats to the United States emanate from nonstate actors at least as much as they do from states. This may become even truer over time, especially as states such as Russia become ever more expert in the use of nonstate or quasi-state actors as proxies for their own policies. The agenda proposed here does focus on norms that apply first and foremost to states, but it addresses this issue in three ways. First, states still have far greater cyber capabilities should they choose to employ them, and thus constraining state cyber aggression is a critical goal and the foundation for any regime of cyber stability. Second, several emerging norms specifically focus on constraining state sponsorship of nonstate actors in this space, state efforts to prevent their territory from being used by such groups, and cooperation in the identification and prosecution of cyber criminals, thus offering an important avenue of mitigation of nonstate cyber threats. Third and finally, the basic principles of any of these norms would apply to nonstate actors as well, providing the basis for international pursuit of groups that engage in destructive operations.

The overarching purpose for a cyber norm agenda of promoting stability among the major cyber powers points to several more specific objectives of the process:

1. Create normative constraints on the most dangerous forms of cyber attack, either in peacetime or as escalation in war.
2. Create a context in which self-defense and resilience measures in cyberspace can be more effective.
3. Create the foundation, through multilateral and civil society coalitions as well as through formal international agreements, for continued and gradual progress toward greater constraints.
4. Gradually and generally raise the diplomatic, economic, and reputational cost of unprovoked cyber aggression that contravenes emerging norms.

In the process, the United States will have to take seriously the fact that Russia and China will have very different objectives in some areas, as noted at the beginning of Chapter Three. The objectives of U.S. efforts to promote stabilizing cyber norms may be initially limited—to create barriers to the most destabilizing forms of cyber aggression—but they can also lay the groundwork for an increasingly common international understanding that cyber aggression beyond established redlines is unacceptable, and costly for those that do so.

An important question is whether a renewed cyber norm agenda attempts to restrain cyber espionage activities. The recent SolarWinds attack, for example, is best viewed as an espionage activity rather than a cyber attack with destructive goals.[9] However, in practical terms, it is not clear whether a cyber-normative regime can survive if its boundaries are drawn too finely. If cyber espionage on the scale of SolarWinds becomes public once every six or 12 months, along with many other examples of general intrusions and information manipulation, it will create a public and official sense of unconstrained behavior in the cyber realm—even if a narrow set of norms are being adhered to.

More broadly, any new regime of constraints on cyber activity could have implications for existing U.S. policy and capabilities in these areas. Given the continuing requirement for deterrence and intelligence, the United States will remain active in the cyber realm, presumably including efforts to gain access to information systems of rivals. In some cases it may perceive an urgent requirement to conduct active cyber operations, for example to short-circuit an imminent attack. Any effort to promote a normative regime must work around U.S. operational requirements.

This need not prevent an effort to build norms around a handful of critical principles, but it does speak to the importance of clarifying what the resulting normative regime is trying to do and what it is not. The United States, for example, reportedly engages in all manner of cyber espionage—indeed, it would be irresponsible of a major power *not* to employ cyber means to gather intelligence critical to its self-defense. Yet some U.S. officials have characterized SolarWinds as an

---

[9] This would have the challenging result of exempting the 2020 SolarWinds hack from an emerging set of norms. On its role as cyber espionage, see Erica Borghard and Jacqueline Schneider, "Russia's Attack Wasn't Cyberwar: That Complicates U.S. Strategy," *Wired*, December 17, 2020.

act of war, and have threatened extreme punishments for the action.[10] In order to make a set of limited norms both credible and feasible, the United States will have to be willing to clarify that it does not view every unwanted adversary action as a violation of its proposed rules for cyberspace, in ways it has been so far hesitant to do. Yet the U.S. reputation as a responsible cyber actor has been compromised by a number of revelations over the last decade, and demonstrating a willingness to live by at least a minimal set of rules is important to sustain U.S. leadership on these issues.

An Overall Strategy for Generating Norms: Catalytic and Multistakeholder

Our analysis of the interests and perspectives of the major cyber actors, the character of norms and the cycle of norm emergence, and the history of cyber norm development highlighted two leading principles of a U.S. cyber norm strategy. First, it should be *catalytic*, seeking to encourage the gradual, sometimes messy process of political and social norm emergence rather than trying to put into place a singular treaty or agreement. Second, it should be *multistakeholder*, working with many public and private actors simultaneously to advance normative consensus on a broad front, and lending support to norm entrepreneurs.

As discussed in Chapter Three, these principles—and many of the specific elements of this strategic approach described below—have characterized elements of U.S. policy on cyber stability and cyber norms since about 2011. Our argument is not that this general approach is entirely new, but that the emphasis in U.S. efforts should shift away from international expert negotiation and toward broader political engagement, as well as toward defining a small handful of normative limits with U.S. competitors and ensuring greater harmony between U.S. norm-promotion efforts and other U.S. activities in cyberspace.

---

[10] David Ignatius, "Russia's Solar Winds Hack Was Espionage, Not an Act of War," *Washington Post*, December 22, 2020.

We derived two important findings from the background on the nature of norms (Chapter Two) and the recent dialogues on cyber norms (Chapter Three). First, norms tend to emerge gradually, as products of state practice, shifting beliefs, and nongovernmental activism as much as formal agreements between states. And second, the current international dialogue on cyber norms remains hampered by fundamental differences in perspective and is not sufficiently mature to allow clear, treaty-like agreements.

These findings lead us to our first broad recommendation for U.S. policy toward cyber norms: to continue to pursue, and where possible expand and deepen, a *catalytic approach*, designed to actively urge forward many different avenues to making progress.[11] The character of norm emergence makes such a gradual, iterative, catalytic approach essential. By their nature, norms are gradually emergent, common agreements on what constitutes legitimate behavior. They can only come into place through an incremental process of interaction and social construction. While norms can eventually be codified in treaties (or in rare instances, treaties that already command wide state support can help to spread norms), they are distinct from formal agreements and cannot be mandated into place. Moreover, as discussed earlier in this report, the differences in perspective among the major cyber actors are so profound as to rule out dramatic, comprehensive, short-term accords.

The United States should therefore intensify its commitment to a strategy that seeks to encourage, underwrite, and sponsor a gradually strengthening regime of cyber norms over time. We offer suggestions below of specific ways to do this. Such a catalytic approach would begin with a strong public reaffirmation of the need for norms, including emotive appeals from high-level policymakers about the damage they could avoid, and a specific enumeration of several rules of conduct that the United States would like to see emerge, and that it intends itself to abide by. But the approach will also involve offering expanded engagement across a wide range of norm entrepreneurs, processes, and sources of analysis, from direct support to NGOs promoting norms to

---

[11] Global Commission on the Stability of Cyberspace, 2019, pp. 15–17.

participation in GGE-like intergovernmental negotiations to endorsement of ideas from partner governments. The general U.S. strategy will therefore involve a wide array of actions to catalyze the emergence of a normative regime by generating political and social demand for such norms rather than hosting a single conference or signing a single treaty.

The approach would envision a loosely linked set of partial agreements, processes, and emergent norms that add up to a strong collective effect.[12] These could include NGO advocacy campaigns; intergovernmental agreements among like-minded states; private-sector conventions; and nongovernmental efforts at detection, notification, and transparency. The nature of the issue, with so many complex subcomponents and stakeholders, and the pervasiveness of the internet, mean that information-security agreements have major ramifications for other issue areas, which would further support such a consultative, collaborative approach.[13]

Such an approach could make modified use of the current U.S. emphasis on international law. Agreements about international legal principles can support the development of norms, but they are not a substitute for it. The United States can pursue a broad-based, comprehensive, and multistakeholder approach while still building multilateral support for the idea that international law proscribes certain behaviors.[14] But norms are ultimately political and social constructs, not legal instruments, and the process of developing and strengthening them will need to recognize this.

One category of U.S. action that will be important, as noted above, is restraint in its own active use of cyber tools, but this may also include restraint in related policies such as democracy promotion through the information networks of authoritarian states. If the United States is unwilling to demonstrate some degree of limits in its own employment of these tools, it will increase the challenge of establishing

---

[12] Nye, 2018, pp. 25–26.

[13] Wolfgang Kleinwächter, "Towards a Holistic Approach for Internet Related Public Policy Making," Hague Center for Strategic Studies: Global Commission on the Stability of Cyberspace Thought Piece, January 2018, pp. 6–8.

[14] Tikk and Kerttunen, 2017, p. 20.

that adversary use of similar tools is illegitimate. This issue will be discussed in greater detail below, in our proposal of the specific content of potential cyber norms the United States should support.

The second general principle that ought to guide a U.S. norm-development strategy is a *multistakeholder* approach. Any strategy for developing cyber norms should continue to work through and with multiple state and nonstate organizations, forums, and processes simultaneously. Cyber issues are not like traditional arms control questions; many different actors, private as well as public, have perspectives and stakes in the issues. And building norms, as we have stressed, is a more gradual and emergent process than singular arms treaties, and requires achieving widespread public support and buy-in. The implication is that, as Alexander Klimburg and Virgilio Almeida have argued:

> the multistakeholder approach is not optional, but mandatory for success. Norms that are only developed and promoted by a single actor or actor group are unlikely to be successful in this space—implementation will only be possible if there is shared ownership, and ownership usually means some form of participation. In practical terms, this means that previously state-only norm processes must have much stronger engagement with the private sector and civil society to be successful.[15]

Within the realm of state action, the United States could begin by forming a close partnership with democracies that have advanced information environments, such as European Union member states Japan, South Korea, Australia, and New Zealand.[16] It could seek to develop an initial set of shared norms among these countries. Doing so could also help to enhance U.S. efforts to revitalize these close partnerships and build increasingly shared perspectives on security challenges, vital for many U.S. foreign and security policy goals. A second step would

---

[15] Alexander Klimburg and V. A. F. Almeida, "Cyber Peace and Cyber Stability: Taking the Norm Road to Stability," IEEE Computer Society, July–August 2019, p. 65.

[16] In late 2020, the European Union was developing a proposal to the incoming U.S. administration to reengage on multilateral cooperation in a number of areas, notably including cybersecurity. See Sam Fleming, Jim Brunsden, and Michael Peel, "EU Proposes Fresh Alliance with U.S. in the Face of the China Challenge," *Financial Times*, November 29, 2020.

be the beginnings of enforcement through conditionality: This coalition could impose conditions on foreign technology firms and partner nations wanting a role in their information environments, requiring that they abide by and support enforcement of the proposed norms.

A multistakeholder strategy must continue to reach beyond state actors, however, and embrace the dozens of major nonstate groups and companies with powerful voices in the cybersecurity realm. These include, most obviously, cybersecurity firms, whose operations provide critical awareness of ongoing threats and practices; software companies with an obvious stake in global cybersecurity (such as Microsoft, which has been a leader in promulgating private-sector cyber norm proposals); social media platforms; and NGOs leading the discussion on cybersecurity and cyber norms. The United States can continue to expand its consultations with such stakeholders in ways that will accelerate the emergence of effective norms and help to build public and international consensus around the core principles the United States identifies, as discussed below.

Major Elements of a U.S. Cyber Norm–Promotion Approach: Findings and Recommendations

As this report establishes, cyber norms have a potentially valuable role to play in helping to stabilize competition in cyberspace that, absent further restraints, has the potential to lead to wider conflict. Particularly in areas where negotiated agreements appear elusive, as the record of negotiation over cyber agreements in Chapter Three demonstrates, norms provide an alternative means of shaping state behavior to avoid actions that may be highly costly or destabilizing. Our analysis suggests that the most promising way forward for the United States is to operate as a catalyst of a broad-based political and social movement supporting robust cyber norms, rather than as the convener of processes designed to put into place formal agreements.

A new U.S. administration must also recognize the significant barriers to decisive progress, and the fact that several U.S. administrations have been pushing the issue for some time with limited success. Merely continuing with the same calls for action is not likely to make progress. This is especially true due to the trend of the United States' own behavior in the cyber realm, which has embraced concepts like "Defend Forward" that seem to legitimize exactly the sort of aggressive cyber espionage, theft, and manipulation that it is trying to brand as irresponsible in the norm dialogue. During the last four years, moreover, the Trump administration cut senior cybersecurity positions in the National Security Council and the State Department, generated friction with allies, and undermined its declared policy through mixed messages and inconsistent actions with key adversaries.

The process of building norms, as discussed in Chapter Two, is a long-term endeavor, one that can potentially continue to embed itself in international dialogue and practice even without fully consistent U.S. behavior. Yet a renewed commitment to abiding by proposed norms is important because of the risks involved in the alternative scenario—one of generalized cyber aggression. An emergent normative regime can also collapse, producing a free-for-all environment of unconstrained behavior. This would be exceptionally dangerous for the United States, especially given its dependence on the information realm and the limitations on the effectiveness of strategies grounded in resilience and deterrence alone.

In order to advance the process of norm building over the next 18 to 24 months, the United States should proceed along three parallel lines:

- Mitigate barriers to progress, and set the context for normative development.
- Continue with well-established U.S. lines of effort to catalyze the general process of norm construction.
- Undertake new, specific, short-term actions to achieve specific outcomes within this time frame.

The last component is especially important to give new form and substance to the process of norm construction: The United States should pick what cyber norms it thinks are most important and then substantially elevate the high-level messaging and political attention it pays to imposing diplomatic and political costs for violations.

Stage 1: Clear the Way for Progress

The first component of the strategy is to remove obvious barriers to making further progress on establishing broadly agreed norms in the cyber realm. Our analysis suggests that this component requires at least two major steps:

- *Make clear that while the U.S. position is that international law applies in cyberspace and prohibits certain actions, it recognizes that not all states agree with that interpretation, and this dispute should not obstruct other progress.* Agreeing to statements of cyber restraint not formally grounded in international law does not necessarily dilute the other U.S. claims. The United States should make clear that the important things are the principles, more so than differing views of the justification for them.
- *Indicate a willingness to constrain certain offensive cyber activities to help build credibility for U.S. diplomacy in this area.* The United States could announce an initial set of standards of conduct for state behavior in the cyber realm that the United States will seek to establish and by which it intends to abide. By offering to "go first" in specifying and abiding by the restrictions on illegitimate behavior in the cyber realm that it proposes, the United States would have the opportunity first to define these restrictions in a manner likely to anchor their future discussion and development, as well as to build diplomatic and political support for the restrictions through its own example.[17]

This second point bears elaboration. If the United States (or U.S. allies and partners) employ offensive cyber means more widely, this risks creating a pattern of state behavior suggesting that any norms in this area will not be reliably observed. While it may be theoretically possible to draw fine distinctions regarding which systems the United States targets in adversaries versus those it believes should be off-limits

---

[17] This recommendation would be in keeping with Jacquelyn Schneider's proposed "No First Use" policy for U.S. offensive cyber operations. See Jacquelyn Schneider. "A Strategic Cyber No-First-Use Policy? Addressing the US Cyber Strategy Problem," *Washington Quarterly*, Vol. 43, No. 2, 2020.

to adversary attack, adversaries (as well as other states and the broader public) may not share or even perceive such distinctions.

U.S. behavior in the cyber realm, as a signaling device of state practice, will be important in shaping the potential for cyber norms. Just as it must do in areas such as nuclear weapons use and threats and the employment of landmines and cluster munitions, the United States will have to weigh the unilateral advantages of certain cyber actions against the damage they could cause to emergent norms. Some degree of cyber restraint will likely be required to promote norms that restrict adversary behavior. Choosing to exercise what could initially be unilateral restraint may at the outset seem ill advised, because doing so eschews short-term advantages for the uncertain benefits of the long-term development of a normative regime. (Short-term advantages might include a greater ability to apply coercive pressure to U.S. adversaries or signal U.S. concern in response to adversary behavior.) But it is also likely essential for progress.

An important step for this effort to build trust, credibility, and leadership should involve a senior-level speech that clearly lays out how the United States conducts cyber operations. This public presentation should seek to draw a sharp line between the activities conducted by the United States and those conducted by adversaries such as Russia, China, the DPRK, and Iran. The speech can emphasize, for instance, the narrow national security purpose of U.S. cyber activities, the extensive legal and other reviews necessary for authorization, the technical restraints built into operations, and the importance of adhering to humanitarian and democratic values within all its cyber conduct.

U.S. cyber programs are highly classified, and so this speech could be an opportunity to improve shared international understanding and provide clarity about how the Department of Defense's (DoD's) activities, especially those conducted under the "defend forward" and "persistent engagement" strategies, relate to the promotion of cyber norms. As much as possible given its operational requirements, the United States should seek to be more transparent about the DoD and the U.S. intelligence community's conduct in cyberspace, why it undertakes the operations it does, and how they are authorized.

Stage 2: Continue Existing Initiatives

In addition to actions designed to clear the way for added progress, the new administration could continue with and enhance various initiatives already underway in the cyber norms area. While perhaps less likely to generate significant new progress on their own, they represent critical investments in the long-term emergence of a normative regime, as described in Chapter Two. These steps could include the following:

- *Publicly reemphasize the importance of emerging norms in this area.* In public speeches and statements from senior officials, the new administration can convey the U.S. commitment to an increasingly effective normative regime to enhance cybersecurity and cyber stability. The new administration could formally endorse the spirit of the GGE process and the 11 basic categories of norms that emerged from its 2015 report and the Paris Call principles, without necessarily endorsing every specific proposal in them. It could also call for action on the three specific areas of focus we recommend above. It can renew its participation in multiple international forums, and seek to lead the multilateral diplomatic process on the issue.
- *Feature cyber norms in discussions with democratic allies and partners on a reinvigorated U.S. multilateralism.* The Biden administration has begun to engage in bilateral and multilateral dialogues with partner democracies to strengthen multilateral approaches to shared challenges. Cybersecurity can be a major early focus of such discussions, with the administration seeking explicit, if initially broad, commitments on key cybernormative initiatives. The United States should work to rebuild its partnerships with foreign governments and to bolster its credibility and leadership among a broad community of stakeholders; cooperation on cyber norms could be a key anchor for regaining trust lost in the past few years. This would continue and build on both bilateral and multilateral cyber norm discussions that have been underway for several years.

  President Biden has called for a Summit of Democracy to "renew the spirit and shared purpose of the nations of the free world."[18] This summit can be used to publicly affirm how critical U.S. goals in cyberspace are widely shared among democracies. The summit could be an important opportunity for the United States to build partnerships related to cyber stability, especially regarding norms related to election processes. The United States should convene sessions at the summit focused on election security with an emphasis on cybersecurity and state cyber conduct in the context of democratic elections.[19]

- *Beyond state practice, support intergovernmental, public-private, and nongovernmental organizations and processes designed to ratify the commitment of various coalitions of stakeholders to emergent cyber norms and expand their public profile and attention.* Continuing to engage with and assist a wide range of stakeholders on emerging cyber norms will help to both strengthen their public and international legitimacy and enlist partners in efforts to broaden and deepen support for these norms in key states. In doing so, the United States and like-minded stakeholders should emphasize the human costs of violations of cyber norms, transforming abstract discussions of stability and escalation risk into the concrete risks that violations of cyber norms pose to the well-being of individuals. NGOs may be better placed to make such arguments to domestic and international publics than the United States government.
- *Act to impose costs on states that violate emerging cyber norms.* Violations of cyber norms have been punished in a variety of ways, with the tools available likely expanding if or when norms become more established. In the early stages, simply naming and shaming violators may be an effective tool in clarifying that a violation did occur, and that the United States views the behavior as illegitimate. Depending on the nature of the violation, economic or diplomatic sanctions may also be appropri-

[18] Joseph R. Biden, Jr., "Why America Must Lead Again: Rescuing U.S. Foreign Policy After Trump," *Foreign Affairs*, March/April 2020.

[19] By focusing relatively narrowly on the importance of election security, and other norms affecting critical infrastructure, as discussed below, this renewed push among democracies should not exacerbate Chinese or Russian concerns regarding their own domestic political systems, as discussed in Chapter Three.

ate.[20] As support for the norm expands, and like-minded states internalize the norms as well, broader-based efforts to impose costs on violators may become feasible.

The Biden administration could pursue this objective by articulating a new cyberspace declaratory policy that clearly describes what cyberspace activities it will not accept and how it will respond to unacceptable behavior. This policy should be clear about how it will respond both to actions that violate cyber norms and also to actions like espionage, that, although may not violate cyber norms, still should elicit a punitive response. This would constitute a natural next step after recent public warnings to U.S. rivals and the consensus declaratory principles in the 2021 GGE and OEWG statements.

Importantly, the Biden administration will have to be prepared to back up its declaratory policy with credible cost imposition. Past administrations have not consistently held adversaries responsible for their cyber activities, and the Trump administration especially undercut cyber deterrence with Russia by failing to criticize its aggression in cyberspace and elsewhere. The United States should use the range of cost-imposition measures it has available on its own, while also working with partners to develop new approaches to jointly hold adversaries accountable.

The United States can also multilateralize this process to a more regular and formal degree than it has so far. Washington and its partners have conducted a variety of coordinated activities to respond to cyber attacks, including shared public attribution, economic sanctions, and cyber crime indictments. These actions have begun to demonstrate a joint capability and willingness to take action against irresponsible cyber actors. However, the efforts are still nascent, and there is room to increase the number of participating actors while also ensuring that the coordinated cost imposition is effective, consistent, and timely. These efforts should not be limited only to governments; they should extend to working with

---

[20] Of note, the cost-imposition strategies we recommend are primarily not themselves in the cyber domain. As such, this approach is consistent with our above recommendation that the United States exercise greater restraint in its own actions in cyberspace.

the private sector on areas such as infrastructure takedowns. The United States will need to invest in building the relationships and processes necessary for operationalizing joint coordination, including by assisting countries that need cybersecurity support.

- *Reaffirm and expand CBMs with Russia and China.* Well before cyber norms can be established, there will remain an urgent need for mechanisms for crisis avoidance and resolution in the cyber realm. Moreover, in the early stages of norm development, the United States is likely to be building agreed rules of the road among value-sharing democracies and other responsible cyber actors. During this time, before Russia and China may have signed onto any restraints, or before they perceive any clear costs to violating the emerging norms, the United States will want to build mechanisms to ease tensions and avoid misunderstanding with its primary cyber competitors. This is especially true because of the growing role of other cyber actors, including North Korea, Iran, and nonstate cyber aggressors: Improved CBMs with Russia and China can help to avoid cyber conflict through misperception, including misperception based on the actions of third parties.

  The United States has already sought to use bilateral forums involving the United States and both Russia and China to exchange and discuss claims of cyber aggression.[21] In 2013 bilateral meetings between the United States and Russia, the two countries agreed to three CBMs for the cyber realm. One, noted above, was an agreement to use the U.S.-Russian Nuclear Risk Reduction Center to enhance transparency and reduce misperceptions during a cyber incident. The others involved creating a formal link between cyber institutes on each side—that is, between computer security incident response teams (CSIRTs), known as the CSIRT-CSIRT link—and the use of a White House-Kremlin hotline in the event of cyber-induced crises.

  Unfortunately, these CBMs do not appear to have helped substantially with cyber stability—though they have arguably not yet

---

[21] For a detailed discussion of this issue, see Erica D. Borghard and Shawn W. Lonergan, "Confidence Building Measures for the Cyber Domain," *Strategic Studies Quarterly*, Vol. 12, No. 3, Fall 2018.

been fully tested, in the sense that there has not yet been a destructive cyber attack that risked significant escalation and required such mechanisms to handle. The cyber realm also has characteristics that make CBMs less directly useful than in traditional military areas: To take one leading example, because so many cyber activities are secret and nonattributable, there is not an opportunity for clear, verifiable constraints on day-to-day activities such as was applied to military exercises in Europe during the Cold War. Many actors in the cyber domain are private, moreover, and would have to be drawn into some CBMs in ways that have not been necessary in past military confidence-building processes.

Nonetheless, the new administration could reaffirm its commitment to a process of CBMs and build on that precedent with more behavior-oriented agreements, including an Incidents-at-Sea-like mechanism specifying rules of engagement for dealing with cyber clashes. CBMs could make contributions in some very specific areas of cyber stability, such as avoiding escalation from third-party attacks designed to mimic cyber aggression by major powers, the need to share information regarding any large-scale ongoing global cyber crisis, and perhaps the mutual observation of components of the global information architecture that are essential to all major cyber actors.

Stage 3: Undertake New Initiatives

Finally, the new administration can develop an agenda of actions designed to make tangible progress within its first two years. These actions include a number of general steps and one major initiative, outlined in a separate section below: identifying a handful of specific norms to which it will seek to gain general assent in the next 18 to 24 months. Other new initiatives could include the following:

- *Organize for cyber norm promotion. Formally establish an institutional home within the U.S. government for the process of cyber-norm development.* Without an accountable office in charge of such a strategy, the strategy is less likely to work. One of the great challenges with cyber issues in the U.S. government is that management of them is fragmented across so many offices, commands, and organizations. Many existing organizations, such as U.S. Cyber Command and even the Cybersecurity and Infrastructure Security Agency at the Department of Homeland Security, focus on active use of cyber means or direct cyber defense. Because the process of norm development is naturally a diplomatic one, the logical department to oversee a cyber norm–development strategy is the Department of State. The U.S. Cyberspace Solarium Commission recommended the creation of a Bureau of Cyberspace Security and Emerging Technologies in the department that would be a natural home for such diplomatic activities.[22] The State Department has already endorsed this idea, and new congressional legislation in 2021 would mandate such a bureau, headed by a new assistant secretary position.[23] It only remains to take the final step and implement the idea.

- *Enunciate bilateral, informal commitments with other powers to refrain from certain categories of cyber aggression in ways that help reinforce emergent norms.*[24] Such commitments could include both understandings with potential rivals or adversaries as well as broader statements of agreement from like-minded allies and partners. Close partnership with the European Union is likely to be essential, as is the integration of other value-sharing democracies.[25]

  The new administration could seek to institutionalize such an ongoing effort at formal commitment to cyber norms. The coordinated efforts among partners to take action against cyber attacks have been ad hoc. However, as these relationships and processes mature, the United States should consider formalizing the collective of actors committed to improving cyber stability

---

[22] U.S. Cyberspace Solarium Commission, 2020, pp. 47–48. Such an initiative would require determining how this office relates to the Global Engagement Center. In October 2020, a senior U.S. State Department official endorsed the idea and noted that the department had announced its intention to create a "Bureau for Cyberspace Security and Emerging Technologies (CSET)"; Ford, "Responding to Modern Cyber Threats," 2020.

[23] Maggie Miller, "House Passes Legislation to Elevate Cybersecurity at the State Department," The Hill, April 20, 2021.

[24] Harold, Libicki, and Cevallos, 2016, pp. 70–77, offered an example of such a bilateral commitment: a mutual pledge to refrain from attacks on critical infrastructure.

[25] Kleinwächter, 2018, pp. 10–11.

under a new "Coalition for Cyber Stability." This coalition should be open to both state and nonstate actors that affirm the normative framework that the United States has promoted, and that are willing to work cooperatively against norms violations. The formation of a coalition would signal to adversaries that the United States and coalition members are serious about their resolve to enforce cyber norms and would be a new focal point for the cyber norms conversations that are stalled at the U.N. It would also be a useful starting point of member states for obtaining formal commitments to the specific cyber norms proposed below.

- *Propose a standing working group with either Russia or China (or both) to allow experts and government officials to discuss issues and slowly build toward limited areas of consensus, and to develop rules of engagement and communication mechanisms to handle cyber disputes.*[26] While existing international negotiations have revealed the limited overlap in existing preferences on cyber issues, continuing robust channels of communication may be an important aspect of gradually gaining Russian and Chinese acceptance, or at least acquiescence, to key elements of emerging cyber norms. One focus of such discussions will likely have to be limits on "cyber active defense" and other practices of anticipatory cyber manipulation undertaken to enhance defensive resilience These dialogues would include efforts to establish cyber CBMs. While formal agreements on key points with Russia and China may not be imminent, maintaining open lines of communication to explain U.S. positions and hear Russian and Chinese concerns will be essential to the long-term goal of gaining their acceptance of, or acquiescence to, restrictions on their behavior. The United States could bill such an effort as an explicit follow-on to the productive dialogues in the 2019–2021 GGE process.
- *Convene new multilateral intergovernmental, and multistakeholder, processes to gather a critical mass of partners in the effort.* The United States should devote resources and diplomatic and political support to the efforts of like-minded groups, both domestically and internationally, that can help make the public case for the importance

[26] This idea is proposed in Harold, Libicki, and Cevallos, 2016, pp. 57–58.

of emerging cyber norms to audiences the United States government may have more difficulty in persuading. One lesson of the nature of norm development is that it is useful to push many initiatives simultaneously. While norms are in the process of emerging, multiple overlapping dialogues, processes, and proposals are useful—rather than harmful—because they strengthen the growing sense of a collective commitment to similar principles.

The Centerpiece of a Renewed Push for Norms: Identifying Specific Normative Constraints for Universal Agreement

As the final component of its new initiatives, the new administration should make a powerful public commitment to the foundational norms at the core of its early effort, while making clear that these are simply initial priorities and do not exhaust the scope of normative constraint that can emerge in this domain. In order to support and catalyze the emergence of cyber norms through the process described above, the United States would of course first need to decide on the content of the norms it wishes to prioritize. This decision is likely to be complex and involve trade-offs between the ideal and the feasible, and between standards the United States is itself willing to abide by and those that could eventually come to restrain the behavior of potential adversaries as well.

The 11 norm areas identified by the 2015 United Nations GGE, discussed in Chapter Three of this report, represent one potential list of norms for consideration, as they represent the most significant multilateral statement of possible constraints so far outlined.[27] They hold the following:

1. States should not knowingly allow their territory to be used for internationally wrongful acts using ICTs.
2. States should not conduct or knowingly support ICT activity that intentionally damages critical infrastructure.

[27] These details are quoted from CCDCOE, "2015 UN GGE Report: Major Players Recommending Norms of Behaviour, Highlighting Aspects of International Law," webpage, undated. For the actual report, see United Nations General Assembly, *Group of Governmental Experts on Developments in the Field of Information and Telecommunications in the Context of International Security*, A/70/174 §, 2015.

3. States should take steps to ensure supply chain security, and should seek to prevent the proliferation of malicious ICT and the use of harmful hidden functions.
4. States should not conduct or knowingly support activity to harm the information systems of another state's computer emergency response teams (CERTs/CSIRTs) and should not use their own teams for malicious international activity.
5. States should respect the U.N. resolutions that are linked to human rights on the internet and to the right to privacy in the digital age.
6. States should cooperate to increase stability and security in the use of ICTs and to prevent harmful practices.
7. States should consider all relevant information in cases of ICT incidents.
8. States should consider how best to cooperate to exchange information, to assist each other, and to prosecute terrorist and criminal use of ICTs.
9. States should take appropriate measures to protect their critical infrastructure.
10. States should respond to appropriate requests for assistance by other states whose critical infrastructure is subject to malicious ICT acts.
11. States should encourage responsible reporting of ICT vulnerabilities and should share remedies for these.

These are phrased very broadly and leave much discussion and negotiation to be performed before more precise and effective norms can be built. The Global Commission on the Security of Cyberspace developed a similar set of proposed norms.[28]

Looking more broadly, the considerations reviewed in this report—including the progress made in international negotiations alongside the broader strategic goals and perspectives of the key states—point to a possible framework, summarized in Table 4.1, for organizing the cyber

---

[28] Global Commission on the Stability of Cyberspace, 2019, pp. 21–22. These, too, are very broad and encompassing. A more specific set was included in Global Commission on the Stability of Cyberspace, 2018.

Table 4.1
Defining the Goals of a Normative Regime: Categories of Threat

Category of Cyber Target	Examples	Potential Principles of Cyber Restraint
Attacks on *essential* societal infrastructure	Energy grids, voting systems, dams and water systems, central governmental functions, foundational financial networks[a]	Comprehensive prohibition on disruption or destruction by electronic means
Attacks on *significant*[b] societal infrastructure	Hospitals,[c] transportation networks and infrastructure, wider business and supply chain networks	Comprehensive prohibition on disruption or destruction by electronic means (in any situation short of total warfare); or prohibition of large-scale, multiple-target attacks
Efforts to manipulate and tamper with the design and development of information systems and networks	Changing software or hardware programming in development or deployment to destabilize information systems and networks	Prohibition on "tampering with products and services in development and production" in ways that "substantially impair the stability of cyberspace"[d]
Cyber-enabled efforts to directly alter electoral outcomes or cause change in government	Manipulation of results in electronic voting systems, direct intervention during period of election (e.g., doxfare) to affect outcome, ongoing cyber-enabled campaigns to threaten regime stability	Complete prohibition on any such activities
Targeted, cyber-enabled socioeconomic interference	Efforts to disrupt operations of the internet of things or decisions reliant on algorithmic processes	Prohibition on large-scale disruption (attacks directed at many nodes in networks with significant collective societal effect)
Cyber-enabled theft of economically significant intellectual property	Theft of major industrial processes or secrets	Prohibition on any cyber-enabled theft based on international standards of intellectual property protection

Table 4.1—Continued

Category of Cyber Target	Examples	Potential Principles of Cyber Restraint
Gradual efforts to undermine broad sociopolitical sovereignty and stability	Social and political interference by broadcasting propaganda or messages directly to citizens, ongoing state-run broadcasting efforts, targeted appeals or activities to foment polarization and extremism in target society	Prohibition on: direct engagement with or support for specific extreme, radical, or antigovernment groups; the direct commandeering of systems for use as botnets;[e] large-scale campaigns of messaging through social media platforms

[a] Maurer, Levite, and Perkovich, 2017.

[b] The distinction in this table between *essential* and *significant* infrastructure is intended to represent a rough gradation in the societal damage that interference with these systems could cause, though the line between the two is an imprecise one. Regardless, below we recommend pursuing norms that would prohibit both categories of attacks.

[c] For evidence of recent randomware attacks on U.S. hospitals, see Ellen Barry and Nicole Perlroth, "Patients of a Vermont Hospital Are Left 'in the Dark' After a Cyberattack," *New York Times*, November 26, 2020.

[d] Global Commission in the Stability of Cyberspace, 2018, p. 9.

[e] Global Commission in the Stability of Cyberspace, 2018, p. 11.

threat activities that could be governed by norms. The table lists these activities by category of cyber target and offers examples of the principles of cyber restraint that could apply in each.

Note that this framework explicitly avoids several categories of cyber activities that would not be governed by an initial normative regime (though these could be brought under more extensive regulation over time). These include

- open, public, attributed statements by one government which could have the intent of influencing sociopolitical events in other countries
- cyber-enabled espionage designed to gather information without causing disruption or destruction
- discrete, one-off cyber attacks on localized individual targets without broad-based societal ramifications

- general state-run propaganda or information broadcasts designed to reach the citizens of other countries (such as Russia Today or Voice of America).

This approach would not focus on social media interference as a primary objective in part because the evidence of the impact of such campaigns remains mixed.

Also, this approach does not initially deal with the many *positive* norms that have been suggested by the GGE and other processes—norms such as good "cyber hygiene" and specific requirements to protect information security. As noted above, the set of 11 basic GGE-proposed norms can continue to serve as a wider set of initiatives that the United States can and should endorse and support. But our analysis suggests the value of a smaller set of more narrowly targeted normative initiatives to gain traction over the next two years.

Several criteria, derived from the proposed objectives described above for a normative effort, can help identify priority normative initiatives. The most escalatory and dangerous forms of cyber attack, for example, deal with essential or highly significant infrastructure and networks critical to the operation of modern societies.[29] While social media–based messaging is of concern, there remains limited evidence about its actual effect,[30] whereas direct intervention in electoral processes can have much more explicit effects on the legitimacy of elections.

Based on considerations of urgency and drawing on lessons from the development of other norms, as described earlier, we have concluded that simpler, more absolute norms—as well as those with relatively clear linkages to human welfare—are more likely to spread and become established. Hence, our analysis suggests the follow-

---

[29] Healey and Jervis, 2020.

[30] For a recent summary of evidence, see Timothy Frye, "Inside Job: The Challenge of Foreign Online Interference in U.S. Elections," War on the Rocks, October 6, 2020. See also Michael J. Mazarr, Abigail Casey, Alyssa Demus, Scott W. Harold, Luke J. Matthews, Nathan Beauchamp-Mustafaga, and James Sladden, *Hostile Social Manipulation: Present Realities and Emerging Trends*, Santa Monica, Calif.: RAND Corporation, RR-2713-OSD, 2019, Chapter Five.

ing three major normative initiatives as promising early focus for U.S. attention:[31]

1. *Complete prohibitions on any cyber attacks on critical infrastructure, either essential or significant as defined above.* Attacks on such systems not only risk destabilizing cycles of retaliation, but they also risk direct, substantial harm to civilians. Establishing that cyber operations to destroy or degrade them are no more legitimate than the use of traditional, kinetic military instruments against the same targets should be a core principle of emerging cyber norms, and like-minded states should treat such actions as proscribed.

   This norm was first proposed by the U.S. government (USG) in 2014, affirmed by the United States and others in the 2015 GGE report, reaffirmed in the 2021 GGE statement, and reiterated in many high-level speeches (e.g., by Secretary Kerry, as noted above). It appears in official statements from countless bilateral and multilateral dialogues. The U.N. General Assembly (in a consensus) has also affirmed that states be guided by it. Moreover, there are very few if any actual violations of the norm, so state practice may already be converging to support this norm.

   That said, the problems with the further establishment and acceptance of the norm are well known. Some critics contend that the United States itself violated this norm with the Stuxnet attack (in 2010, before the later norm-building effort), and it otherwise reportedly possesses cyber tools that could damage critical infrastructure. Many governments do not trust that the United States will actually be constrained by this norm. Internationally, the growing prominence of ransomware attacks has drawn in sectors that clearly fall under definitions of critical infrastructure, including hospitals and energy grids, and if states cannot rein in profit-seeking hackers, this norm could dissipate over time.

---

[31] While worthy of attention and further consideration for the future, the other categories outlines in Table 4.1, including norms around broader information campaigns or economic activity, are either more difficult to construct relatively simple, universal rules around (i.e., they are less promising), or they represent less acute threats to stability in interstate relations (i.e., they are less urgent).

Defining critical infrastructure in a way that can be universally accepted also remains a challenge. The United States has identified 16 critical infrastructure sectors, which are quite broad and have expanded over time. As one example, the United States could seek to include major financial institutions in this category. Three scholars have recommended a cyber norm requiring that a "State must not conduct or knowingly support any activity that intentionally manipulates the integrity of financial institutions' data and algorithms wherever they are stored or when in transit."[32]

2. *Prohibitions on direct interference in or manipulation of election and political processes.* The possibility of foreign actors using cyber means to directly undermine the mechanics of elections reflects a potential existential threat to the viability of democratic political systems. While current adversary capabilities to do so should not be overstated, the United States and its democratic allies and partners should aggressively promote the view that any such attacks are fundamentally illegitimate and will be punished.[33]

   In 2017, the USG publicly designated election infrastructure as part of critical infrastructure.[34] As such, the USG has stated that the norm it supports prohibiting attacks on critical infrastructure also prohibits cyber operations that disrupt or degrade election infrastructure. The USG has sought to publicly communicate the importance of this norm, including to the Russians through the Nuclear Risk Reduction Center, and it has claimed that it would impose costs on violators, including during the Trump administration.

   But special emphasis on this norm appears warranted given its importance for the United States in particular, and other

---

[32] Maurer, Levite, and Perkovich, 2017.

[33] There is already some emerging state practice in this area to build on. See William M. Arkin, Ken Dilanian, and Cynthia McFadden, "What Obama Said to Putin on the Red Phone About the Election Hack," NBC News, December 19, 2016.

[34] U.S. Department of Homeland Security, "Statement by Secretary Jeh Johnson on the Designation of Election Infrastructure as a Critical Infrastructure Subsector," Office of the Press Secretary, January 6, 2017.

democratic states more generally. In emphasizing this norm, the United States will need to deal with contrary arguments made by states such as Russia and China that a norm in this area should instead be expanded to include any interference in the politics of other countries, to include nongovernmental civil society or democracy promotion efforts. While future negotiations over those issues are in theory possible, the United States—and other like-minded democracies—should make clear that it views interference in electoral processes themselves as a separate issue, and that it will treat any violations as being attacks of the most serious nature.

3. *Prohibitions on activity designed to intentionally and substantially damage the availability or integrity of the public core of the internet*, including the basic Domain Name System as well as central server locations and primary avenues of data transmission. This principle exists in both the GGE and Paris Call sets of principles and reflects an effort to prevent large-scale attacks on the operation of the internet.

    Though this norm has been discussed for many years in cyber norms forums, it is not one that the United States has actually affirmed to date. One hesitation may be a U.S. desire to reserve freedom of action to conduct cyber operations on the infrastructure of the internet's public core. For instance, compromising the public core might be the best or only way for the United States to disrupt an attack on its election system under certain circumstances.

    China has previously engaged in cyber attacks on the public core, including (perhaps inadvertent) attacks on the Domain Name System and the Border Gateway Protocol. Indeed, this is a key component of China's attempt to censor the domestic internet and control content. Russia might see value in these types of operations too. U.S. promotion of this norm may therefore require both greater promises of self-restraint than it has been willing to make to date and a willingness to "go first" and accept that adversaries may continue to contemplate such actions until norms prohibiting them can become firmly established.

These areas of focus represent what we assess to be the most promising and urgent places to begin in efforts to promote cyber norms. Should these initial efforts gain traction, the United States could also expand its efforts on a wider front to establish a more comprehensive set of cyber norms, first among democracies and then more broadly. Combined with the investment in catalytic, multistakeholder efforts towards cyber norm emergence as described above, they would constitute an agenda designed to make as much progress as possible toward greater cyber stability in an admittedly constraining international context.

Bibliography

Achten, Nele, "New U.N. Debate on Cybersecurity in the Context of International Security," Lawfare Blog, September 30, 2019. As of June 4, 2021: https://www.lawfareblog.com/new-un-debate-cybersecurity-context-international-security

Arkin, William M., Ken Dilanian, and Cynthia McFadden, "What Obama Said to Putin on the Red Phone About the Election Hack," NBC News, December 19, 2016. As of December 4, 2020: https://www.nbcnews.com/news/us-news/what-obama-said-putin-red-phone-about-election-hack-n697116

Barry, Ellen, and Nicole Perlroth, "Patients of a Vermont Hospital Are Left 'in the Dark' After a Cyberattack," *New York Times*, November 26, 2020. As of June 4, 2021: https://www.nytimes.com/2020/11/26/us/hospital-cyber-attack.html

Biden, Joseph R., Jr., "Why America Must Lead Again: Rescuing U.S. Foreign Policy After Trump," *Foreign Affairs*, March/April 2020. As of January 22, 2021: https://www.foreignaffairs.com/articles/united-states/2020-01-23/why-america-must-lead-again

Björkdahl, Annika, "Norms in International Relations: Some Conceptual and Methodological Reflections," *Cambridge Review of International Affairs*, Vol. 15, No. 1, 2002, pp. 9–23.

Borghard, Erica D., and Shawn W. Lonergan, "Confidence Building Measures for the Cyber Domain," *Strategic Studies Quarterly*, Vol. 12, No. 3, Fall 2018, pp. 10–49.

———, "To Defend Forward, the U.S. Must Strengthen the Cyber Mission Force," Lawfare Blog, March 13, 2020. As of May 23, 2021: https://www.lawfareblog.com/defend-forward-us-must-strengthen-cyber-mission-force

Borghard, Erica, and Jacqueline Schneider, "Russia's Attack Wasn't Cyberwar: That Complicates U.S. Strategy," *Wired*, December 17, 2020. As of May 23, 2021: https://www.wired.com/story/russia-solarwinds-hack-wasnt-cyberwar-us-strategy/

Brantly, Aaron, and Liam Collins, "A Bear of a Problem: Russian Special Forces Perfecting Their Cyber Capabilities," Association of the United States Army, November 28, 2018. As of December 1, 2020:
https://www.ausa.org/articles/bear-problem-russian-special-forces-perfecting-their-cyber-capabilities

Buchanan, Ben, and Robert D. Williams, "A Deepening U.S.-China Cybersecurity Dilemma," Lawfare Blog, October 24, 2018. As of December 1, 2020:
https://www.lawfareblog.com/deepening-us-china-cybersecurity-dilemma

Cardenas, Sonia, "Norm Collision: Explaining the Effects of International Human Rights Pressure on State Behavior," *International Studies Review*, Vol. 6, No. 2, 2004, pp. 213–231.

Carnegie Endowment for International Peace, "Cyber Norms Index and Timeline," last updated January 2021. As of January 20, 2021:
https://carnegieendowment.org/publications/interactive/cybernorms

Carpenter, R. Charli., "Vetting the Advocacy Agenda: Network Centrality and the Paradox of Weapons Norms," *International Organization*, Vol. 65, No. 1, January 2011, pp. 69–102.

CCDCOE, "2015 UN GGE Report: Major Players Recommending Norms of Behaviour, Highlighting Aspects of International Law," webpage, undated. As of May 24, 2021:
https://ccdcoe.org/incyder-articles/2015-un-gge-report-major-players-recommending-norms-of-behaviour-highlighting-aspects-of-international-law/

———, "An Updated Draft of the Code of Conduct Distributed in the United Nations—What's New?" undated. As of June 4, 2021:
https://ccdcoe.org/incyder-articles/an-updated-draft-of-the-code-of-conduct-distributed-in-the-united-nations-whats-new/

Charap, Samuel, "Strategic Sderzhivanie: Understanding Contemporary Russian Approaches to 'Deterrence,'" *Security Insights*, No. 62, September 2020. As of December 1, 2020:
https://www.marshallcenter.org/en/publications/security-insights/strategic-sderzhivanie-understanding-contemporary-russian-approaches-deterrence-0

Charney, Scott, Erin English, Aaron Kleiner, Nemanja Malisevic, Angela McKay, Jan Neutze, and Paul Nicholas, *From Articulation to Implementation: Enabling Progress on Cybersecurity Norms*, Microsoft, white paper, June 2016.

Checkel, Jeffrey T., "The Constructivist Turn in International Relations Theory," *World Politics*, Vol. 50, No. 2, 1998, pp. 324–348.

Conley, Heather A., and Jean-Baptiste Jeangène Vilmer, *Successfully Countering Russian Election Interference*, Center for Strategic and International Studies, June 21, 2018. As of December 1, 2020:
https://www.csis.org/analysis/successfully-countering-russian-electoral-interference

Council of Europe, "Chart of Signatures and Ratifications of Treaty 185, Convention on Cybercrime," undated. As of May 17, 2021: https://www.coe.int/en/web/conventions/full-list/-/conventions/treaty/185/signatures?p_auth=qCJbWwDb

Craig, Amanda N., Scott J. Shackelford, and Janine S. Hiller, "Proactive Cybersecurity: A Comparative Industry and Regulatory Analysis," *American Business Law Journal*, Vol. 52, No. 4, 2015, pp. 721–787.

Crowe, Philip, "Will a Big Election Win for Ardern Reshape New Zealand's China Policy?" *World Politics Review*, October 1, 2020. As of December 1, 2020: https://www.worldpoliticsreview.com/articles/29098/will-a-big-ardern-win-in-new-zealand-elections-reshape-her-china-policy

Cyber Tech Accord, "Cybersecurity Tech Accord," 2018. As of June 4, 2021: https://cybertechaccord.org/accord/

———, "Cybersecurity Tech Accord Celebrates Its Second Anniversary," February 25, 2020. As of June 25, 2020: https://cybertechaccord.org/cybersecurity-tech-accord-celebrates-its-second-anniversary/

Day, Jennifer Cheeseman, Alex Janus, and Jessica Davis, *Computer and Internet Use in the United States: 2003*, Special Studies, Current Population Reports, U.S. Census Bureau, October 2005.

Deibert, Ronald, "Towards a Cyber Security Strategy for Global Civil society?" Canada Centre for Global Security Studies, 2011. As of June 4, 2021: https://www.giswatch.org/en/freedom-expression/towards-cyber-security-strategy-global-civil-society

Delegation of the United States of America, *Other Disarmament Issues and International Security Segment of Thematic Debate in the First Committee of the Sixty-Seventh Session of the United Nations General Assembly*, U.S. Department of State, November 2, 2012. As of June 4, 2021: https://2009-2017.state.gov/t/avc/rls/200050.htm

Denison, Benjamin, "Where US Sees Democracy Promotion, Russia Sees Regime Change," Russia Matters, July 29, 2020. As of December 1, 2020: https://www.russiamatters.org/analysis/where-us-sees-democracy-promotion-russia-sees-regime-change

Economy, Elizabeth C., "The Great Firewall of China: Xi Jinping's Internet Shutdown," *The Guardian*, June 29, 2018. As of December 1, 2020: https://www.theguardian.com/news/2018/jun/29/the-great-firewall-of-china-xi-jinpings-internet-shutdown

Eichensehr, Kristen, "International Cyber Governance: Engagement Without Agreement?" Just Security, February 2, 2015. As of June 4, 2021: https://www.justsecurity.org/19599/international-cyber-governance-engagement-agreement/

Faesen, Louk, Tim Sweijs, Alexander Klimburg, Conor MacNamara, and Michael Mazarr, *From Blurred Lines to Red Lines: How Countermeasures and Norms Shape Hybrid Conflict*, Hague Centre for Strategic Studies, October 2020. As of June 4, 2021: https://hcss.nl/report/from-blurred-lines-to-red-lines-how-countermeasures-and-norms-shape-hybrid-conflict/

Fidler, David P., "Final Acts of the World Conference on International Telecommunications," *International Legal Materials*, Vol. 52, No. 3, 2013, pp. 843–860. As of June 4, 2021: https://doi.org/10.5305/intelegamate.52.3.0843

Finnemore, Martha, and Kathryn Sikkink, "International Norm Dynamics and Political Change," *International Organization*, Vol. 52, No. 4, 1998, pp. 887–917. As of June 24, 2020: www.jstor.org/stable/2601361

Fischerkeller, Michael P., and Richard J. Harknett, "Deterrence Is Not a Credible Strategy for Cyberspace (and What Is)," Institute for Defense Analyses, 2017. As of May 23, 2021: https://www.ida.org/-/media/feature/publications/w/we/welch-awards-2018-research-notes-fall-2019/welch-awards-2018-research-notes-fall-2019-article-1.ashx?la=en&hash=C725B2340ABA96463DBAF3D298E7671A

———, *Persistent Engagement, Agreed Competition, Cyberspace Interaction Dynamics, and Escalation*, Institute for Defense Analyses, May 2018. As of May 23, 2021: https://www.ida.org/-/media/feature/publications/p/pe/persistent-engagement-agreed-competition-cyberspace-interaction-dynamics-and-escalation/d-9076.ashx

Fleming, Sam, Jim Brunsden, and Michael Peel, "EU Proposes Fresh Alliance with U.S. in the Face of the China Challenge," *Financial Times*, November 29, 2020.

Florini, Ann, "The Evolution of International Norms," *International Studies Quarterly*, Vol. 40, No. 3, 1996, pp. 363–389.

Ford, Christopher, "Cyberspace Security Diplomacy: Deterring Aggression in Turing's Monument," remarks at the Foreign Service Institute, May 13, 2020. As of June 4, 2021: https://2017-2021.state.gov/cyberspace-security-diplomacy-deterring-aggression-in-turings-monument/index.html

———, "Rules, Norms, and Community: Arms Control Discourses in a Changing World," remarks at European Union Conference on Nonproliferation, December 13, 2019. As of June 4, 2021: https://2017-2021.state.gov/rules-norms-and-community-arms-control-discourses-in-a-changing-world/index.html

———, "Responding to Modern Cyber Threats with Diplomacy and Deterrence," speech at the Center for Strategic and International Studies, October 19, 2020. As of June 4, 2021: https://2017-2021.state.gov/responding-to-modern-cyber-threats-with-diplomacy-and-deterrence/index.html

Frye, Timothy. "Inside Job: The Challenge of Foreign Online Interference in U.S. Elections," War on the Rocks, October 6, 2020. As of June 4, 2021:
https://warontherocks.com/2020/10/inside-job-the-challenge-of-foreign-online-influence-in-u-s-elections/

Gilli, Andrea, and Mauro Gilli. "Why China Has Not Caught Up Yet: Military-Technological Superiority and the Limits of Imitation, Reverse Engineering, and Cyber Espionage," *International Security*, Vol. 43, No. 3, 2019, pp. 141–189.

GIP Digital Watch Observatory, "UN GGE and OEWG: GIP Digital Watch Observatory for Internet Governance and Digital Policy," February 14, 2020. As of June 4, 2021:
https://dig.watch/processes/un-gge

Gizewski, Peter, "From Winning Weapon to Destroyer of Worlds: The Nuclear Taboo in International Politics," *International Journal*, Vol. 51, No. 3, 1996, pp. 397–419.

Global Commission on the Stability of Cyberspace, *Norm Package Singapore*, December 16, 2018. As of June 4, 2021:
https://cyberstability.org/research/singapore_norm_package/

———, *Advancing Cyberstability*, Final Report, Hague Center for Strategic Studies and EastWest Institute, November 2019.

Gold, Josh, "The First Ever Global Meeting on Cyber Norms Holds Promise, but Broader Challenges Remain," Council on Foreign Relations Blog, September 30, 2019. As of June 4, 2021:
https://www.cfr.org/blog/first-global-meeting-cyber-norms

———, "A Cyberspace 'FIFA' to Set Rules of the Game? UN States Disagree at Second Meeting," Council on Foreign Relations Blog, March 2, 2020. As of June 4, 2021:
https://www.cfr.org/blog/cyberspace-fifa-set-rules-game-un-states-disagree-second-meeting

Goldman, Emily O., "From Reaction to Action: Adopting a Competitive Posture in Cyber Diplomacy," *Texas National Security Review*, Fall 2020. As of June 4, 2021:
https://tnsr.org/2020/09/from-reaction-to-action-adopting-a-competitive-posture-in-cyber-diplomacy/

Goldsmith, Jack, "What Explains the U.S.-China Cyber 'Agreement'?" Lawfare Blog, September 26, 2015. As of December 1, 2020:
https://www.lawfareblog.com/what-explains-us-china-cyber-agreement

Goldsmith, Jack, and Stuart Russell, *Strengths Become Vulnerabilities: How a Digital World Disadvantages the United States in Its International Relations*, Hoover Institution, Aegis Series Paper 1806, 2018. As of December 1, 2020:
https://www.belfercenter.org/sites/default/files/files/publication/381100534-strengths-become-vulnerabilities.pdf

Gompert, David C., Astrid Stuth Cevallos, and Cristina L. Garafola, *War with China: Thinking Through the Unthinkable*, Santa Monica, Calif.: RAND Corporation, RR-1140-A, 2016. As of December 1, 2020: https://www.rand.org/pubs/research_reports/RR1140.html

Government of the Russian Federation, "Prime Minister Vladimir Putin Meets with Secretary General of the International Telecommunications Union Hamadoun Toure," 2011. As of June 4, 2021: http://archive.government.ru/eng/docs/15601/print/

Grant, Thomas, "Russia's Invasion of Ukraine: What Does International Law Have to Say?" Lawfare Blog, August 25, 2015. As of October 13, 2020: https://www.lawfareblog.com/russias-invasion-ukraine-what-does-international-law-have-say

Grigsby, Alex, "The End of Cyber Norms," *Survival*, Vol. 59, No. 6, 2017, pp. 109–22. As of June 4, 2021: https://doi.org/10.1080/00396338.2017.1399730

Group of 20, "G20 Leaders' Communiqué Agreed in Antalya," Antalya Summit, November 15–16, 2015. As of May 23, 2021: http://g20.org.tr/g20-leaders-commenced-the-antalya-summit/

Hansen, Toran, "The Campaign to Ban Landmines," *Peace Review*, Vol. 16, No. 3, 2004, pp. 365–370.

Harknett, Richard J., and Max Smeets, "Cyber Campaigns and Strategic Outcomes," *Journal of Strategic Studies*, Vol. 20, 2020, pp. 1–34. As of June 4, 2021: https://www.tandfonline.com/doi/full/10.1080/01402390.2020.1732354

Harold, Scott W., "The U.S.-China Cyber Agreement: A Good First Step," *Cipher Brief*, July 31, 2016. As of December 1, 2020: https://www.thecipherbrief.com/article/tech/the-u-s-china-cyber-agreement-a-good-first-step

Harold, Scott W., Martin C. Libicki, and Astrid Stuth Cevallos, *Getting to Yes with China in Cyberspace*, Santa Monica, Calif.: RAND Corporation, RR-1335-RC, 2016. As of May 17, 2021: https://www.rand.org/pubs/research_reports/RR1335.html

Harris, Shane, "Obama Stares Down China on Cyberspying," *Daily Beast*, September 25, 2015. As of December 1, 2020: https://www.thedailybeast.com/obama-stares-down-china-on-cyberspying?ref=scroll

Healey, Jason, and Robert Jervis, "The Escalation Inversion and Other Oddities of Situational Cyber Stability," *Texas National Security Review*, Fall 2020. As of June 4, 2021: https://tnsr.org/2020/09/the-escalation-inversion-and-other-oddities-of-situational-cyber-stability/

Huang, Yukon, and Jeremy Smith, "China's Record on Intellectual Property Rights Is Getting Better and Better," *Foreign Policy*, October 16, 2019. As of March 3, 2021:
https://foreignpolicy.com/2019/10/16/china-intellectual-property-theft-progress/

Human Rights Watch, "Russia: Growing Internet Isolation, Control, Censorship," webpage, June 18, 2020. As of December 1, 2020:
https://www.hrw.org/news/2020/06/18/russia-growing-internet-isolation-control-censorship#

Hurel, Louise Marie, and Luisa Cruz Lobato, "Unpacking Cyber Norms: Private Companies as Norm Entrepreneurs," *Journal of Cyber Policy*, Vol. 3, No. 1, 2018, pp. 61–76. As of June 4, 2021:
https://doi.org/10.1080/23738871.2018.1467942

Ignatius, David, "Russia's Solar Winds Hack Was Espionage, Not an Act of War," *Washington Post*, December 22, 2020. As of January 21, 2021:
https://www.washingtonpost.com/opinions/russias-solarwinds-hack-was-espionage-not-an-act-of-war/2020/12/22/ffa8f88a-4498-11eb-b0e4-0f182923a025_story.html

International Campaign to Ban Landmines, "Treaty Status," undated. As of October 22, 2020:
http://www.icbl.org/en-gb/the-treaty/treaty-status.aspx

International Committee of the Red Cross, *Anti-Personnel Landmines: Friend or Foe? A Study of the Military Use and Effectiveness of Anti-Personnel Mines*, 1996. As of October 22, 2020:
https://www.icrc.org/en/publication/0654-anti-personnel-landmines-friend-or-foe-study-military-use-and-effectiveness-anti

International Telecommunications Union, International Telecommunication Regulations, WATTC-88 §, 1989.

———, *Final Acts of the World Conference on International Telecommunications*, 2012.

Jensen, Eric Talbot, "The Tallinn Manual 2.0: Highlights and Insights International Justice: Where We Stand, Where We Fall, and Where We Need to Be," *Georgetown Journal of International Law*, Vol. 48, No. 3, 2016, pp. 735–778. As of June 4, 2021:
https://heinonline.org/HOL/P?h=hein.journals/geojintl48&i=743

Joint Force Development, *Cyberspace Operations, Joint Publication 3-12*, Joint Chiefs of Staff, June 8, 2018.

Kania, Elsa B., and John K. Costello, "The Strategic Support Force and the Future of Chinese Information Operations," *Cyber Defense Review*, Vol. 3, No. 1, 2018, pp. 105–122.

Katzenstein, Mary Fainsod, *The Culture of National Security: Norms and Identity in World Politics*, New York: Columbia University Press, 1996.

Kelion, Leo, "US Resists Losing Control of Internet Passing to UN Agency," BBC News, August 3, 2012. As of June 4, 2021:
https://www.bbc.com/news/technology-19106420

Kerry, John, "An Open and Secure Internet: We Must Have Both," remarks at Korea University, U.S. Department of State, May 18, 2015. As of June 4, 2021:
https://2009-2017.state.gov/secretary/remarks/2015/05/242553.htm

Kleinwächter, Wolfgang, "Towards a Holistic Approach for Internet Related Public Policy Making," Hague Center for Strategic Studies: Global Commission on the Stability of Cyberspace Thought Piece, January 2018.

Klimburg, Alexander, "Building a Pluralist Future for the Internet," Atlantic Council of the United States, September 3, 2014. As of June 4, 2021:
https://www.atlanticcouncil.org/commentary/article/building-a-pluralist-future-for-the-internet/

Klimburg, Alexander, *The Darkening Web: The War for Cyberspace*, New York: Penguin, 2017.

Klimburg, Alexander, ed., *National Cybersecurity Framework Manual*, Tallinn: NATO Cooperative Cyber Defence Centre of Excellence, 2012.

Klimburg, Alexander, and V. A. F. Almeida, "Cyber Peace and Cyber Stability: Taking the Norm Road to Stability," IEEE Computer Society, July–August 2019. As of June 4, 2021:
https://ieeexplore.ieee.org/document/8874985

Koh, Harold Hongju, "International Law Cyberspace," paper presented at CYBERCOM Inter-Agency Legal Conference, Ft. Meade, Md., 2012.

Korzak, Elaine, "International Law and the UN GGE Report on Information Security," Just Security, December 2, 2015. As of June 4, 2021:
https://www.justsecurity.org/28062/international-law-gge-report-information-security/

———, "UN GGE on Cybersecurity: The End of an Era?" *The Diplomat*, July 31, 2017. As of June 4, 2021:
https://thediplomat.com/2017/07/un-gge-on-cybersecurity-have-china-and-russia-just-made-cyberspace-less-safe/

———, "What's Ahead in the Cyber Norms Debate?" Lawfare Blog, March 16, 2020. As of June 4, 2021:
https://www.lawfareblog.com/whats-ahead-cyber-norms-debate

Krasner, Stephen D., "Structural Causes and Regime Consequences: Regimes as Intervening Variables," *International Organization*, Vol. 36, No. 2, 1982, pp. 185–205.

Kreps, Sarah, "The Shifting Chessboard of International Influence Operations," Brookings Institution, September 22, 2020. As of December 1, 2020:
https://www.brookings.edu/techstream/the-shifting-chessboard-of-international-influence-operations/

Kuerbis, Brenden, and Farzaneh Badiei, "Mapping the Cybersecurity Institutional Landscape," *Digital Policy, Regulation and Governance*, Vol. 19, No. 6, 2017, pp. 466–492. As of June 17, 2020:
https://doi.org/10.1108/DPRG-05-2017-0024

Landler, Mark, and Stephen Castle, "'No One' Protected British Democracy from Russia, U.K. Report Concludes," *New York Times*, July 21, 2020. As of December 1, 2020:
https://www.nytimes.com/2020/07/21/world/europe/uk-russia-report-brexit-interference.html

Landmine and Cluster Munitions Monitor, *China: Mine Ban Policy*, October 15, 2020. As of July 8, 2021:
http://www.the-monitor.org/en-gb/reports/2020/china/mine-ban-policy.aspx

———, *Russian Federation: Mine Ban Policy*, December 18, 2019. As of October 22, 2020:
http://www.the-monitor.org/en-gb/reports/2019/russian-federation/mine-ban-policy.aspx

Lebovic, James H., and Erik Voeten, "The Cost of Shame: International Organizations and Foreign Aid in the Punishing of Human Rights Violators," *Journal of Peace Research*, Vol. 46, No. 1, 2009, pp. 79–97.

Levitsky, Steven, and Lucan Way, "International Linkage and Democratization," *Journal of Democracy*, Vol. 16, No. 3, 2005, pp. 20–34.

Libicki, M., "The Coming of Cyber Espionage Norms," paper presented at 9th International Conference on Cyber Conflict (CyCon), Tallinn, Estonia, May 30–June 2, 2017.

Liubchenkova, Natalia, "There's Only One Way to Tackle Ukraine's Infestation of Mines . . . Slowly," *Euronews*, March 13, 2019. As of October 22, 2020:
https://www.euronews.com/2019/01/28/mine-ridden-areas-in-eastern-ukraine-face-deadly-threat

Lynn, William J., III, "Defending a New Domain," *Foreign Affairs*, May 30, 2014. As of June 4, 2021:
https://www.foreignaffairs.com/articles/united-states/2010-09-01/defending-new-domain

Maizland, Lindsay, "China's Repression of Uighurs in Xinjiang," Council on Foreign Relations, June 30, 2020. As of October 13, 2020:
https://www.cfr.org/backgrounder/chinas-repression-uighurs-xinjiang

Makinen, Julie, "Chinese Censorship Costing U.S. Tech Firms Billions in Revenue," *Los Angeles Times*, September 22, 2015. As of December 1, 2020:
https://www.latimes.com/business/la-fi-china-tech-20150922-story.html

MANRS.org, "Mutually Agreed Norms for Routing Security (MANRS)," September 20, 2019. As of June 4, 2021:
https://www.manrs.org/

Markoff, Michele G., "Explanation of Position at the Conclusion of the 2016–2017 UN Group of Governmental Experts (GGE) on Developments in the Field of Information and Telecommunications in the Context of International Security," U.S. Department of State, June 23, 2017. As of May 23, 2021: https://2017-2021.state.gov/explanation-of-position-at-the-conclusion-of-the-2016-2017-un-group-of-governmental-experts-gge-on-developments-in-the-field-of-information-and-telecommunications-in-the-context-of-international-sec/index.html

———, "Remarks to the UN Group of Governmental Experts on Advancing Responsible State Behavior in Cyberspace in the Context of International Security," United States Mission to the United States, March 28, 2021. As of June 16, 2021: https://usun.usmission.gov/remarks-to-the-un-group-of-governmental-experts-on-advancing-responsible-state-behavior-in-cyberspace-in-the-context-of-international-security/

Marks, Joseph, "U.S. Makes New Push for Global Rules in Cyberspace," *Politico*, May 5, 2015. As of June 4, 2021: https://www.politico.com/story/2015/05/us-makes-new-push-for-global-rules-in-cyberspace-117632

Matsnev, Oleg, "Kremlin Moves Toward Control of Internet, Raising Censorship Fears," *New York Times*, April 11, 2019. As of December 1, 2020: https://www.nytimes.com/2019/04/11/world/europe/russia-internet-censorship.html

Maurer, Tim, "Private Companies Take the Lead on Cyber Security," War on the Rocks, May 4, 2018. As of June 4, 2021: https://warontherocks.com/2018/05/private-companies-take-the-lead-on-cyber-security/

Maurer, Tim, and Jason Healey, "What It'll Take to Forge Peace in Cyberspace," Carnegie Endowment for International Peace, March 20, 2017. As of June 4, 2021: https://carnegieendowment.org/2017/03/20/what-it-ll-take-to-forge-peace-in-cyberspace-pub-68351

Maurer, Tim, Ariel Levite, and George Perkovich, *Toward a Global Norm Against Manipulating the Integrity of Financial Data*, Carnegie Endowment for International Peace, March 27, 2017. As of May 24, 2021: https://carnegieendowment.org/2017/03/27/toward-global-norm-against-manipulating-integrity-of-financial-data-pub-68403

Mazanec, Brian M., "Towards a Cyber War Taboo? A Framework to Explain the Emergence of Norms for the Use of Force in Cyberspace," *National Cybersecurity Institute Journal*, Vol. 1, No. 1, 2014, pp. 56–70.

Mazarr, Michael J., Ryan Michael Bauer, Abigail Casey, Sarah Heintz, and Luke J. Matthews, *The Emerging Risk of Virtual Societal Warfare: Social Manipulation in a Changing Information Environment*, Santa Monica, Calif.: RAND Corporation, RR-2714-OSD, 2019. As of May 25, 2021: https://www.rand.org/pubs/research_reports/RR2714.html

Mazarr, Michael J., Abigail Casey, Alyssa Demus, Scott W. Harold, Luke J. Matthews, Nathan Beauchamp-Mustafaga, and James Sladden, *Hostile Social Manipulation: Present Realities and Emerging Trends*, Santa Monica, Calif.: RAND Corporation, RR-2713-OSD, 2019. As of May 17, 2021:
https://www.rand.org/pubs/research_reports/RR2713.html

McCarthy, Kieren, "Watch Your MANRS: Akamai, Amazon, Netflix, Microsoft, Google, and Pals Join Internet Routing Security Effort," *The Register*, 2020. As of June 4, 2021:
https://www.theregister.com/2020/03/31/manrs_cdns/

McConnell, Bruce, Pavel Sharikov, and Maria Smekalova, "Suggestions on Russia-U.S. Cooperation in Cybersecurity," Russian International Affairs Council and East-West Institute, Policy Brief No. 11, May 2017.

McKay, Angela, Paul Nicholas, Jan Neutze, and Kevin Sullivan, "International Cybersecurity Norms: Reducing Conflict in an Internet-Dependent World," Microsoft Corporation, 2014. As of June 4, 2021:
https://download.microsoft.com/download/7/6/0/7605D861-C57A-4E23-B823-568CFC36FD44/International_Cybersecurity_%20Norms.pdf

McKune, Sarah, "An Analysis of the International Code of Conduct for Information Security," Citizen Lab, September 28, 2015. As of June 4, 2021:
https://citizenlab.ca/2015/09/international-code-of-conduct/

Miller, Maggie, "House Passes Legislation to Elevate Cybersecurity at the State Department," The Hill, April 20, 2021. As of June 16, 2021:
https://thehill.com/policy/cybersecurity/549385-house-passes-legislation-to-elevate-cybersecurity-at-the-state?rl=1

Ministry of Foreign Affairs of the People's Republic of China, "Address by Vice Foreign Minister Li Baodong at the Opening Ceremony of the International Workshop on Information and Cyber Security," June 5, 2014. As of June 4, 2021:
https://www.fmprc.gov.cn/mfa_eng/wjbxw/t1162458.shtml

Mueller, Robert S., III, *Report on the Investigation into Russian Interference in the 2016 Presidential Election*, U.S. Department of Justice, March 2019. As of December 1, 2020:
https://www.justice.gov/storage/report.pdf

Nakamitsu, Izumi, "Group of Governmental Experts on Advancing Responsible State Behaviour in Cyberspace in the Context of International Security," United Nations Office for Disarmament Affairs, December 9, 2019.

Nobel Prize, "The Nobel Peace Prize 1997," webpage, undated. As of October 22, 2020:
https://www.nobelprize.org/prizes/peace/1997/summary/

North Atlantic Council, "Statement on Russia's Failure to Comply with the Intermediate-Range Nuclear Forces (INF) Treaty," February 1, 2019. As of October 13, 2020:
https://www.nato.int/cps/en/natohq/news_162996.htm

Nye, Joseph S., "Normative Restraints on Cyber Conflict," Harvard University Belfer Center, August 2018.

Oliker, Olga, Christopher S. Chivvis, Keith Crane, Olesya Tkacheva, and Scott Boston, *Russian Foreign Policy in Historical and Current Context: A Reassessment*, Santa Monica, Calif.: RAND Corporation, PE-144-A, 2015. As of December 1, 2020: http://www.rand.org/pubs/perspectives/PE144.html

Osula, Anna-Maria, and Henry Rõigas, "Introduction," in Osula and Rõigas, eds., *International Cyber Norms: Legal, Policy and Industry Perspectives*, Tallinn: NATO Cooperative Cyber Defence Centre of Excellence, 2016, pp. 11–22.

Paris Call for Trust and Security in Cyberspace, homepage, November 12, 2018. As of May 23, 2021: https://pariscall.international/en/

Parker, Emily, "Russia Is Trying to Copy China's Approach to Internet Censorship," *Slate*, April 4, 2017. As of December 1, 2020: https://slate.com/technology/2017/04/russia-is-trying-to-copy-chinas-internet-censorship.html

Pfeifer, Ezekiel, "Why Doesn't Russia Censor the Internet Like China?" Institute of Modern Russia, April 15, 2015. As of December 1, 2020: https://imrussia.org/en/nation/2229-why-doesnt-russia-censor-the-internet-like-china

Pomerleau, Mark, "New Authorities Mean Lots of New Missions at Cyber Command," FifthDomain.com, May 8, 2019. As of May 23, 2021: https://www.fifthdomain.com/dod/cybercom/2019/05/08/new-authorities-mean-lots-of-new-missions-at-cyber-command/

Porche, Isaac R., III, Christopher Paul, Chad C. Serena, Colin P. Clarke, Erin-Elizabeth Johnson, and Drew Herrick, *Tactical Cyber: Building a Strategy for Cyber Support to Corps and Below*, Santa Monica, Calif.: RAND Corporation, RR-1600-A, 2017. As of November 10, 2020: https://www.rand.org/pubs/research_reports/RR1600.html

Powers, Shawn M., and Michael Jablonski, *The Real Cyber War: The Political Economy of Internet Freedom*, Champaign: University of Illinois Press, 2015.

Rosert, Elvira, "Norm Emergence as Agenda Diffusion: Failure and Success in the Regulation of Cluster Munitions," *European Journal of International Relations*, Vol. 25, No. 4, 2019, pp. 1103–1131.

Rutherford, Kenneth R., "The Evolving Arms Control Agenda: Implications of the Role of NGOs in Banning Antipersonnel Landmines," *World Politics*, Vol. 53, No. 1, 2000, pp. 74–114.

Sacks, Samm, "Beijing Wants to Rewrite the Rules of the Internet," *The Atlantic*, June 18, 2018. As of December 1, 2020: https://www.theatlantic.com/international/archive/2018/06/zte-huawei-china-trump-trade-cyber/563033/

Sanger, David E., and Steven Lee Myers, "After a Hiatus, China Accelerates Cyberspying Efforts to Obtain U.S. Technology." *New York Times*, November 29, 2018. As of June 4, 2021:
https://www.nytimes.com/2018/11/29/us/politics/china-trump-cyberespionage.html

Sanger, David E., Nicole Perlroth, and Julian E. Barnes, "Billions Spent on U.S. Defenses Failed to Detect Giant Russian Hack," *New York Times*, December 16, 2020. As of June 4, 2021:
https://www.nytimes.com/2020/12/16/us/politics/russia-hack-putin-trump-biden.html

Schmitt, Michael N., "Computer Network Attack and the Use of Force in International Law: Thoughts on a Normative Framework Essays on the Laws of War and War Crimes Tribunals in Honor of Teleford Taylor," *Columbia Journal of Transnational Law*, Vol. 37, No. 3, 1998, pp. 885–938. As of June 4, 2021:
https://papers.ssrn.com/sol3/papers.cfm?abstract_id=1603800

———, "Cyber Operations and the Jud Ad Bellum Revisited Norman J. Shachot Symposium," *Villanova Law Review*, Vol. 56, No. 3, 2011, pp. 569–606. As of June 4, 2021:
https://digitalcommons.law.villanova.edu/cgi/viewcontent.cgi?article=1019&context=vlr

———, "The Sixth United Nations GGE and International Law in Cyberspace," Just Security, June 10, 2021. As of June 16, 2021:
https://www.justsecurity.org/76864/the-sixth-united-nations-gge-and-international-law-in-cyberspace/

Schneider, Jacquelyn, "A Strategic Cyber No-First-Use Policy? Addressing the US Cyber Strategy Problem," *Washington Quarterly*, Vol. 43, No. 2, 2020, pp. 159–175.

Searight, Amy, "Countering China's Influence Operations: Lessons from Australia," Center for Strategic and International Studies, May 8, 2020. As of December 1, 2020:
https://www.csis.org/analysis/countering-chinas-influence-operations-lessons-australia

Segal, Adam, "The U.S.-China Cyber Espionage Deal One Year Later," Council on Foreign Relations, September 28, 2016. As of December 1, 2020:
https://www.cfr.org/blog/us-china-cyber-espionage-deal-one-year-later

Stevens, Tim, "A Cyberwar of Ideas? Deterrence and Norms in Cyberspace," *Contemporary Security Policy*, Vol. 33, No. 1, 2012, pp. 148–170. As of June 4, 2021:
https://doi.org/10.1080/13523260.2012.659597

Sukumar, Arun M., "The UN GGE Failed. Is International Law in Cyberspace Doomed as Well?" Lawfare Blog, July 4, 2017. As of June 4, 2021:
https://www.lawfareblog.com/un-gge-failed-international-law-cyberspace-doomed-well

Sunstein, Cass R., "Social Norms and Social Roles," *Columbia Law Review*, Vol. 96, No. 4, 1996, pp. 903–968.

Tan, J. S., "Big Tech Embraces New Cold War Nationalism," *Foreign Policy*, August 27, 2020. As of December 1, 2020: https://foreignpolicy.com/2020/08/27/china-tech-facebook-google/

Tannenwald, Nina, "The Nuclear Taboo: The United States and the Normative Basis of Nuclear Non-Use," *International Organization*, Vol. 53, No. 3, 1999, pp. 433–468.

———, "Stigmatizing the Bomb: Origins of the Nuclear Taboo," *International Security*, Vol. 29, No. 4, 2005, pp. 5–49.

———, "Nuclear Weapons and the Vietnam War," *Journal of Strategic Studies*, Vol. 29, No. 4, 2006, pp. 675–722.

Tikk, Eneken, and Mika Kerttunen, *The Alleged Demise of the UN GGE: An Autopsy and Eulogy*, New York: Cyber Policy Institute, 2017.

Tucker, Eric, "US Charges Chinese Officials in Cyberspying Case," AP News, May 19, 2014. As of June 4, 2021: https://apnews.com/50f9ddfd20e6416194fc119d4200bfb8

United Nations, *Convention on Prohibitions or Restrictions on the Use of Certain Conventional Weapons Which May Be Deemed to Be Excessively Injurious or to Have Indiscriminate Effects: Protocol on Prohibitions or Restrictions on the Use of Mines, Booby-Traps and Other Devices: Protocol II*, October 10, 1980. As of October 22, 2020: https://www.unog.ch/80256EE600585943/(httpPages)/4F0DEF093B4860B4C1257180004B1B30?OpenDocument

———, "Letter Dated 12 September 2011 from the Permanent Representatives of China, the Russian Federation, Tajikistan, and Uzbekistan to the United Nations Addressed to the Secretary-General," September 14, 2011.

———, "Letter Dated 9 January from the Permanent Representatives of China, Kazakhstan, Kyrgyzstan, the Russian Federation, Tajikistan, and Uzbekistan to the United Nations Addressed to the Secretary-General," January 9, 2015.

———, "First Committee Approves 27 Texts, Including 2 Proposing New Groups to Develop Rules for States on Responsible Cyberspace Conduct," Meetings Coverage, November 8, 2018. As of June 4, 2021: https://www.un.org/press/en/2018/gadis3619.doc.htm

———, "Regional Consultations Series of the Group of Governmental Experts on Advancing Responsible State Behaviour in Cyberspace in the Context of International Security." United Nations, December 2019.

United Nations 73rd Session First Committee, "Advancing Responsible State Behaviour in Cyberspace in the Context of International Security," Resolution 73/37, October 18, 2018.

———, "Developments in the Field of Information and Telecommunications in the Context of International Security," Resolution 73/27, October 29, 2018.

United Nations General Assembly, *Developments in the Field of Information and Telecommunications in the Context of International Security*, 53/70 A/RES/53/70 §, 1999.

———, *Group of Governmental Experts on Developments in the Field of Information and Telecommunications in the Context of International Security*, A/65/201 §, 2010.

———, *Group of Governmental Experts on Developments in the Field of Information and Telecommunications in the Context of International Security*, A/68/98 §, 2013.

———, *Group of Governmental Experts on Developments in the Field of Information and Telecommunications in the Context of International Security*, A/70/174 §, 2015.

———, *Developments in the Field of Information and Telecommunications in the Context of International Security*, 71/28 A/RES/71/28 §, 2016.

United Nations Group of Governmental Experts (UN GGE), "Report of the Group of Governmental Experts on Advancing Responsible State Behaviour in Cyberspace in the Context of International Security," May 28, 2021. As of June 16, 2021: https://front.un-arm.org/wp-content/uploads/2021/06/final-report-2019-2021-gge-1-advance-copy.pdf

United Nations Office for Disarmament Affairs, "Developments in the Field of Information and Telecommunications in the Context of International Security," undated. As of June 4, 2021:
https://www.un.org/disarmament/ict-security/

———, "Fact Sheet: Developments in the Field of Information and Telecommunications in the Context of International Security," July 2019. As of June 4, 2021:
https://unoda-web.s3.amazonaws.com/wp-content/uploads/2019/07/Information-Security-Fact-Sheet-July-2019.pdf

United Nations Open-Ended Working Group, "(2nd Meeting) Open-Ended Working Group on Developments in the Field of Information and Telecommunications in the Context of International Security—Second Substantive Session (10–14 February 2020)," United Nations Web TV, 2020. As of May 22, 2021:
https://media.un.org/en/asset/k13/k13vs7v1kt

———, "(3rd Meeting) Open-Ended Working Group on Developments in the Field of Information and Telecommunications in the Context of International Security—Second Substantive Session (10–14 February 2020)," United Nations Web TV, 2020. As of May 22, 2021:
https://media.un.org/en/asset/k1z/k1zwzw8wa2

———, "(4th Meeting) Open-Ended Working Group on Developments in the Field of Information and Telecommunications in the Context of International Security—Second Substantive Session (10–14 February 2020)," United Nations Web TV, 2020. As of June 4, 2021:
https://media.un.org/en/asset/k18/k18w6jq6eg

———, "(8th Meeting) Open-Ended Working Group on Developments in the Field of Information and Telecommunications in the Context of International Security—Second Substantive Session (10–14 February 2020)," United Nations Web TV, 2020. As of June 4, 2021:
https://media.un.org/en/asset/k1j/k1jdh1iqnt

U.S. Census Bureau, "Computer and Internet Access in the United States: 2010," 2010. As of June 4, 2021:
https://www.census.gov/data/tables/2010/demo/computer-internet/computer-use-2010.html

U.S. Cyberspace Solarium Commission, *Final Report*, March 2020.

U.S. Department of Homeland Security, "Statement by Secretary Jeh Johnson on the Designation of Election Infrastructure as a Critical Infrastructure Subsector," Office of the Press Secretary, January 6, 2017. As of June 4, 2021:
https://www.dhs.gov/news/2017/01/06/statement-secretary-johnson-designation-election-infrastructure-critical

U.S. Department of Justice, "First U.S.-China High-Level Joint Dialogue on Cybercrime and Related Issues Summary of Outcomes," December 2, 2015. As of June 2, 2021:
https://www.justice.gov/opa/pr/first-us-china-high-level-joint-dialogue-cybercrime-and-related-issues-summary-outcomes-0

U.S. Department of State, "U.S. Intervention at the World Conference on International Telecommunications," December 13, 2012. As of June 4, 2021:
https://2009-2017.state.gov/r/pa/prs/ps/2012/12/202037.htm

———, "Joint Statement on Advancing Responsible State Behavior in Cyberspace," September 23, 2019. As of June 4, 2021:
https://www.state.gov/joint-statement-on-advancing-responsible-state-behavior-in-cyberspace/

U.S. Secretary of Defense, *DoD Policy on Landmines*, January 31, 2020. As of October 22, 2020:
https://media.defense.gov/2020/Jan/31/2002242359/-1/-1/1/DOD-POLICY-ON-LANDMINES.PDF

Valeriano, Brandon, Benjamin Jensen, and Ryan C. Maness, *Cyber Strategy: The Evolving Character of Power and Coercion*, New York: Oxford University Press, 2018.

Varenikova, Maria, "Battling Wildfire and Pandemic, Ukraine Faces a New Foe: Landmines," *New York Times*, October 3, 2020. As of October 22, 2020:
https://www.nytimes.com/2020/10/03/world/europe/ukraine-wildfires-landmines.html

Vietnam Veterans of America Foundation, "An Open Letter to President Clinton," *New York Times*, April 3, 1996.

Voo, Julia, Irfan Hemani, Simon Jones, Winnona DeSombre, Dan Cassidy, and Anina Schwarzenbach, *National Cyber Power Index 2020*, Belfer Center for Science and International Affairs, September 2020. As of February 26, 2021: https://www.belfercenter.org/publication/national-cyber-power-index-2020

Ward, Alex, "How the U.S. Government Attack Happened, and What It Means, Explained by an Expert," *Vox*, December 18, 2020. As of June 4, 2021: https://www.vox.com/22187866/usa-cyber-hack-solar-winds-microsoft

Weber, Valentin, "Why China's Internet Censorship Model Will Prevail over Russia's," Council on Foreign Relations Blog, December 12, 2017. As of December 1, 2020: https://www.cfr.org/blog/why-chinas-internet-censorship-model-will-prevail-over-russias

Wexler, Lesley, "The International Deployment of Shame, Second-Best Responses, and Norm Entrepreneurship: The Campaign to Ban Landmines and the Landmine Ban Treaty," *Arizona Journal of International and Comparative Law*, Vol. 20, 2003, pp. 561–606.

White House, *International Strategy for Cyberspace: Prosperity, Security, and Openness in a Networked World*, May 2011. As of May 23, 2021: https://obamawhitehouse.archives.gov/sites/default/files/rss_viewer/international_strategy_for_cyberspace.pdf

———, "Fact Sheet: U.S.-Russian Cooperation on Information and Communications Technology Security," Office of the Press Secretary, June 17, 2013. As of June 4, 2021: https://obamawhitehouse.archives.gov/the-press-office/2013/06/17/fact-sheet-us-russian-cooperation-information-and-communications-technol

———, "Fact Sheet: Changes to U.S. Anti-Personnel Landmine Policy," September 23, 2014. As of October 22, 2020: https://obamawhitehouse.archives.gov/the-press-office/2014/09/23/fact-sheet-changes-us-anti-personnel-landmine-policy

———, "Fact Sheet: President Xi Jinping's State Visit to the United States," Office of the Press Secretary, September 25, 2015. As of June 4, 2021: https://obamawhitehouse.archives.gov/the-press-office/2015/09/25/fact-sheet-president-xi-jinpings-state-visit-united-states

———, "Remarks by President Obama and President Xi of the People's Republic of China in Joint Press Conference," Office of the Press Secretary, September 25, 2015. As of June 4, 2021: https://obamawhitehouse.archives.gov/the-press-office/2015/09/25/remarks-president-obama-and-president-xi-peoples-republic-china-joint

———, *National Cyber Strategy of the United States*, September 2018. As of December 1, 2020: https://trumpwhitehouse.archives.gov/wp-content/uploads/2018/09/National-Cyber-Strategy.pdf

White House Office of Trade and Manufacturing Policy, *How China's Economic Aggression Threatens the Technologies and Intellectual Property of the United States and the World*, June 2018. As of December 1, 2020:
https://www.hsdl.org/?abstract&did=812268

Wittner, Lawrence S., *The Struggle Against the Bomb: Volume One, One World or None: A History of the World Nuclear Disarmament Movement Through 1953*, Stanford, Calif.: Stanford University Press, 1993.

World Conference on International Telecommunications, "WCIT-12 Final Acts Signatories," International Telecommunications Union, December 14, 2012. As of June 4, 2021:
http://www.itu.int/osg/wcit-12/highlights/signatories.html

Zetter, Kim, "Fixing Democracy: The Election Security Crisis and Solutions for Mending It," *Texas National Security Review*, Fall 2020. As of June 4, 2021:
https://tnsr.org/2020/09/fixing-democracy-the-election-security-crisis-and-solutions-for-mending-it/